POKÉMON KNITTING

BRING YOUR FAVORITE POKÉMON TO LIFE WITH 20 CUTE KNITTING PATTERNS

Katie Boyette

DAVID & CHARLES
—PUBLISHING—

www.davidandcharles.com

A DAVID AND CHARLES BOOK

©2024 Pokémon. ©1995–2024 Nintendo/ Creatures Inc./
GAME FREAK inc. TM, ®, and character names are trademarks
of Nintendo.

David and Charles is an imprint of David and Charles, Ltd
Suite A, Tourism House, Pynes Hill, Exeter, EX2 5WS

First published in the UK and USA in 2024

A catalogue record for this book is available from the British
Library.

ISBN-13: 9781446314142

FSC
www.fsc.org
MIX
Paper | Supporting
responsible forestry
FSC® C179467

Printed in China by Guangzhou Yimi Paper Co, Ltd, for:
David and Charles, Ltd
Suite A, Tourism House, Pynes, Hill, Exeter, EX2 5WS

10 9 8 7 6 5 4 3 2 1

Publishing Director: Ame Verso
Designer: Insight Design Concepts Ltd
Technical Editor: Carole Ibbetson
Photography: Wayfaring Wanderer
Packager: BlueRed Press Ltd

David and Charles publishes high-quality books on a wide range
of subjects. For more information visit
www.davidandcharles.com.

Share your makes with us on social media using
#dandcbooks and follow us on Facebook and Instagram
by searching for @dandcbooks.

Figures on cover not to scale.

IMPORTANT

These patterns are not intended as Pokémon for children under
three years old because of the small parts. You may also want to
consider using washable yarns and stuffing.

CONTENTS

INTRODUCTION

My name is Katie Boyette. I live in the Blue Ridge Mountains of Western North Carolina with my husband Dave, our beloved cats Freddie and Curtis, and our rooster Fabio.

I first learned to knit at the age of thirty. It was actually my third attempt at knitting, with the previous two times ending in frustration. What was different the third time? The internet's growing selection of videos and other resources from which to learn. Also, instead of casting on the standard scarf as a first project, I decided to make a very simple cardigan for my then two-year-old. It may sound like an ambitious beginning, but I found the challenge was what made me stick with the project—I was finally knitting something I was actually excited about.

My second knitting project was a basic toy cat. Surprisingly, the completion of the cat project inspired a love of knitting Pokémon that carries through to the present. And what's not to love? Knitted Pokémon are quick and sometimes challenging projects that hold your interest, they're great for using up leftovers from the yarn stash, and they make great gifts!

When I was asked to work on knitted Pokémon, I was admittedly very excited. Both of my kids as well as my nephews, all grown now, are longtime fans of Pokémon, and I simply couldn't resist the opportunity to earn some "cool points" with my family. I'd like to especially thank my youngest, Sage, and my nephew, Alex, for their encouragement and input while embarking on this journey.

If you are holding this book, chances are that either you or a loved one is a fan of Pokémon. Maybe you're an experienced knitter, and these patterns will be a breeze for you. Or perhaps you're a novice, and these Pokémon represent your biggest knitting challenge yet. My advice to you is to dive right in! In my experience, you're much more likely to finish a challenging project that you're excited about rather than an easy project that bores you.

SKILL LEVELS

The projects in this book are divided into three categories: beginner, intermediate and advanced. If you are just learning to knit, I encourage you to start with one of the beginner projects. If you have some knitting under your belt, I'd suggest trying any of the projects in this book. Knitting your favorite Pokémon is great motivation for learning a new knitting technique.

BEGINNER PROJECTS

For these projects you will need to know the basic knitting skills, such as casting on, knitting, purling, increases, and decreases. You will also need to be able to knit in the round. All the Pokémon in this book are knit in the round to simplify shaping and to limit the amount of seaming you'll need to do at the finish.

Knitting in the round can feel a bit cumbersome the first time you attempt it, but once you get going, you will appreciate how much simpler and faster it is to complete projects. You'll find directions in the book explaining this technique. There are also many resources online worth exploring.

INTERMEDIATE PROJECTS

These projects include all the skills mentioned above, plus some additional construction, and in some cases, some simple colorwork.

ADVANCED PROJECTS

The advanced projects include all the skills named above, but also include some advanced techniques like short row shaping.

DIFFICULTY LEVELS

BEGINNER

INTERMEDIATE

ADVANCED

TOOLS AND MATERIALS

BRUSH

For fluffy elements, such as Eevee's collar, a brush to comb out the strands of yarn is needed. This can be a wire felt brush, or even a toothbrush.

CROCHET HOOK

For Pokémon with fluffy elements, such as Eevee, you will need a crochet hook to pull strands of fluffed yarn through the stitches. Any crochet hook sized US size 1 (2.5mm) or smaller will work.

EMBROIDERY NEEDLE

Some patterns require a sewing or embroidery needle. Any small sewing needle will work. I find curved embroidery needles particularly helpful when working with Pokémon.

EMBROIDERY THREAD

For some characters embroidery thread is needed to create certain elements, such as mouths or eyebrows. Use multi-stranded embroidery thread. You can adjust the thickness of the thread by removing strands as needed—or even add more to thicken the stitch.

FELT

Acrylic or wool felt is used to create the Pokémon's eyes, paw pads, etc. This felt can be found at any craft store, although an even greater variety of colors can be found online. Either wool or acrylic will work equally well.

GLUE

Fabric glue should be used to attach the felt elements to the knitted Pokémon. Use a thin layer, or apply small dots with a toothpick or needle. Keep in mind this glue is permanent and can't be removed once applied.

NEEDLES

The patterns in this book require a set of US 5 (3.75mm) double-pointed needles (DPNs). Most patterns require five needles. I prefer bamboo needles. If you are skilled in the magic loop technique, you can substitute a US 5 (3.75mm) circular needle instead.

PINS

Sewing pins are useful to hold the knitted pieces in place while you seam. Choose pins with large heads that won't slide between knitted stitches.

SCISSORS

You will need scissors to cut yarn and felt pieces. Small sharp scissors work best.

SEWING THREAD

Sewing thread is required for certain embroidery elements. It is used to hold the embroidery thread in place when couching. Be sure to match the color of your sewing thread to the embroidery thread.

STITCH MARKERS

For the patterns in this book, I recommend using removable stitch markers. If the end of round is at the edge of the needle, you can attach the marker to the yarn instead of the needle.

STUFFING

Polyester toy stuffing is readily available at any store with a craft supply area. Any brand will work, but I do find the cheaper brands tend to produce lumpier Pokémon.

YARN

For the patterns in this book, I recommend using a 100% wool yarn in DK weight. A few patterns also require yarn in fingering Weight. I find wool yarn provides a nice soft stitch definition, and the wool strands bind together to hold shapes well while stuffing. My preferred yarn is Cascade 220. It is a high-quality, affordable wool yarn that comes in a large variety of colors. The recommended colors in each pattern are chosen to match the Pokémon's official colors.

YARN NEEDLE

You will need a yarn needle to seam together the pieces of your Pokémon. A large sewing needle with a blunt end is best; these are often called tapestry needles.

HOW TO USE THIS BOOK

At the beginning of this book, you'll find information on the tools and materials needed to complete the Pokémon patterns, as well as explanations for the techniques used. The patterns are organized in order of difficulty. Each pattern also includes templates for cutting out felt details.

HOW TO READ PATTERNS

Each section of the Pokémon pattern begins with the yarn color and number of stitches to cast on. Most of these Pokémon are knit in the round. These pattern lines begin with "Round." Some pieces are worked flat, meaning working back and forth. These lines begin with "Row."

All of these Pokémon patterns are completed using double pointed needles. In most cases, there are instructions on how many stitches to keep on each needle. Following this guideline will make the instructions easier to follow. If you are an advanced knitter who prefers using the magic loop technique, you can place stitch markers at these intersections instead.

Abbreviations are used for all patterns in the book. You will want to familiarize yourself with the abbreviations located in the reference table at right.

Each line in the pattern indicates instructions for every stitch in one completed round or row. In some cases, there will be a repeated sequence, indicated by brackets. For example, you may see the pattern line: [K1, k2tog, k2, k2tog, k1] 4 times. (32 sts) In this example, you would complete the sequence over each section of ten stitches, decreasing two stitches each time, ending with a total of thirty-two stitches, eight stitches in each sequence.

At the end of each line, a number in brackets indicates how many stitches you should have on your needles. Be sure to complete each round as written, and to check your stitch count regularly.

SUBSTITUTE YARNS

You can use any DK weight yarn for these patterns. Wool, acrylic, and cotton are all acceptable, but wool provides the tightest stitch definition, which is preferable for these Pokémon. Most patterns use a skein or less, so these Pokémon are a great way to use up your yarn stash. For elements that need to be fluffed, you can substitute wool roving if desired.

KNITTING ABBREVIATIONS

approx.	approximately
dec	decrease
inc	increase
k	knit
k2tog/k3tog	knit two/three stitches together as one
kfb	knit into the front and back of one stitch
LH	left hand
M1	make one
p	purl
p2tog/p3tog	purl two/three stitches together as one
pfb	purl into the front and back of one stitch
PM	place marker
RH	right hand
RS	right side of work
skpo	slip 1, knit 1, pass slipped st over
sl k2tog psso	slip 1, knit 2 together, pass slipped st over decrease
SM	slip marker
SSK	slip slip knit
st(s)	stitch(es)
WS	wrong side of work
W+Tk/p	wrap and turn knit/purl
stockinette stitch	knit on RS rows, purl on WS rows
garter stitch	knit every row
[ ]	indicates a repeat sequence

US TO UK TERMS

US	UK
bind off	cast off
stockinette	stocking stitch
filling	stuffing
gauge	tension

NEEDLE CONVERSION CHART

US	Metric	UK
1.5	2.5mm	18
2	2.75mm	12
-	3mm	11
3	3.25mm	10
4	3.5mm	-
5	3.75mm	9
6	4mm	8
7	4.5mm	7
8	5mm	6

TECHNIQUES

CASTING ON

For the patterns in this book, I recommend using the long tail cast on method. If you are knitting in the round, cast on all stitches onto one needle, then divide over the other needles.

BIND OFF

To bind off, knit the first two stitches on your row/round, then pull the first stitch over the second stitch. Repeat till all stitches are bound off. Break the yarn, and pull the tail through the remaining stitch.

SEWING UP

I recommend using a mattress stitch for seaming together all knitted pieces in this book. The mattress stitch seam creates an invisible join, using this stitch will create a ridge on the inside of your work which can give your garment more structure.

FILLING

Use polyester toy filling/stuffing to fill your Pokémon. Take chunks of stuffing and fluff it out before inserting it into the toy. I recommend placing pieces around the perimeter, leaving a cavity in the middle to fill as you go. This will prevent lumpiness. Then fill the middle until the toy is firm, but not overfilled. If you overfill, just pull some stuffing back out.

SCULPTING

Once the toy is fully filled, you can begin sculpting it into shape. If you have smaller detail areas, such as a nose, add a little blob of stuffing to that area and gently squeeze into shape. Once the toy is fully stuffed and secured, gently manipulate the stuffing. This will allow you to control the roundness of a character's head, for instance. If you accidentally flatten a shape, you can fluff it out again by inserting a small knitting needle between the stitches and gently pulling outward.

STITCHES

GENERAL

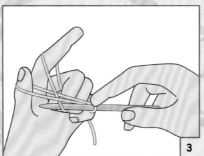

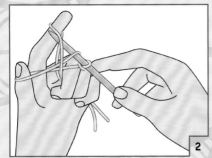

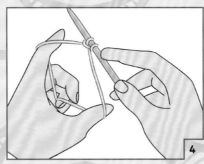

LONG TAIL CAST ON

1. Pull a long length of yarn from yarn ball, and create a slipknot in the middle. Slide slipknot onto the needle. This is the first stitch.
2. Loop yarn tails around fingers as pictured. Insert needle upward through the back loop and pull backside of the front loop forward with the tip of the needle.
3. Pull tip of the needle down through the second loop.
4. Pull both tails tight, securing stitch on needle. Repeat for remaining stitches.

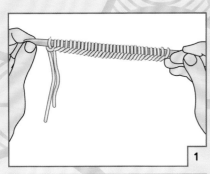

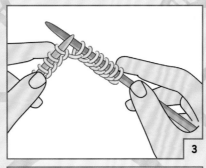

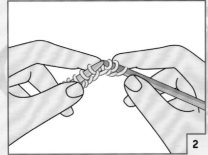

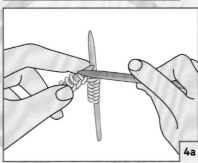

WORKING IN THE ROUND WITH DPNS

1. Cast the required number of stitches onto one DPN.
2. Slide a quarter of the stitches onto a second needle.
3. Slide the next quarter of the stitches onto a third needle.
4. Slide the next quarter of the stitches onto a fourth needle.

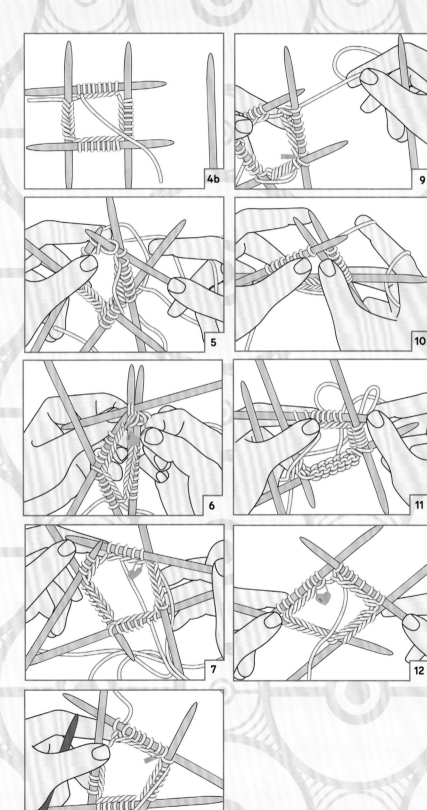

5. Insert your empty DPN into the first cast on stitch, work the yarn around and complete the stitch.

6. Mark the beginning of the round between two needles by inserting a stitch marker into the edge of the knitting.

7. Continue to work across the stitches on the first needle.

8. As you finish each DPN, you will end up with a new empty needle shown here as the darker needle, left.

9. Picking up the working yarn, knit the first stitch, pulling it gently to secure the join between the stitches in the round.

10. Place a stitch marker at the base of the first stitch to mark the beginning of the round.

11. Knit stitches across the first needle.

12. Rotate work to continue knitting the stitches along the second needle. Continue rotating work and knitting the next needle as you go, moving the stitch marker along as needed.

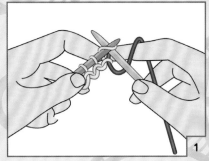

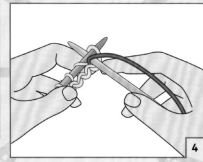

KNIT

1. Insert the tip of the right needle into the front loop of the first stitch on the left from left to right.
2. Wrap working yarn around the tip of the right needle.
3. Pull loop through stitch.
4. Pull the new stitch forward while letting the old stitch fall off the left needle.

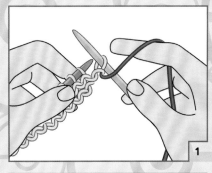

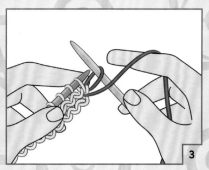

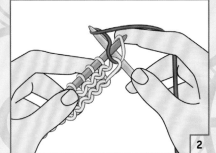

PURL

1. Insert tip of right needle into the front loop of the first stitch on the left from right to left.
2. Wrap working yarn around the tip of the right needle.
3. Pull loop through stitch.
4. Pull the new stitch forward while letting the old stitch fall off the left needle.

SHAPING

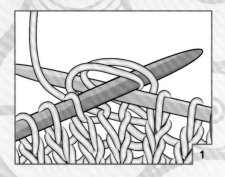

K2TOG

1. Insert the tip of the needle through the next two stitches knit-wise. Wrap working yarn around tip of right needle. Pull loop through. Let both stitches fall off the left needle.

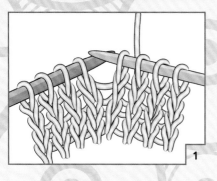
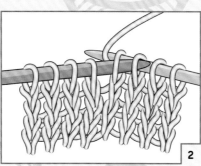

SSK

1. Slip the next two stitches knit-wise onto the right needle.
2. Insert left needle purl-wise into both slipped stitches and knit together.

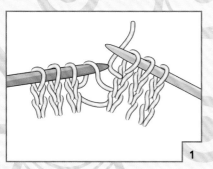
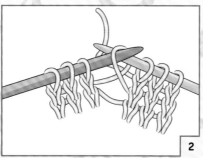

M1

1. Using the tip of the right needle, lift the bar between the next two stitches and place it on the left needle.
2. Knit through the back loop of the lifted stitch and slide off the needle.

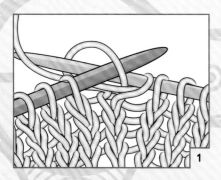

KFB

1. Knit the next stitch, but leave the old stitch on the left needle. Slip the right needle through the back loop of the left stitch. Pull the tail of the yarn through to create a new stitch. Slip the old stitch off the left needle.

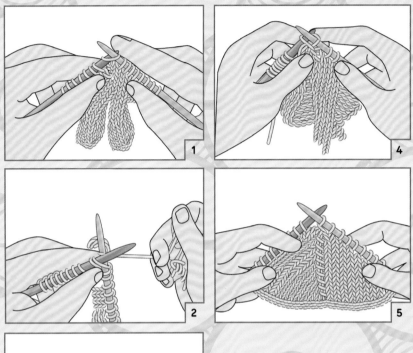

SL K2TOG PSSO

1. Slip one stitch from the left needle to the right needle knit-wise.

2. Knit the next two stitches on the left needle together.

3. Using the tip of the left needle, lift the slipped stitch up and over the first stitch.

4. Pull the lifted stitch off the right needle and pull it to secure.

5. Continue knitting along the left needle.

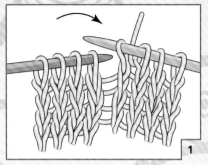

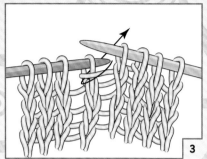

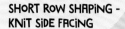

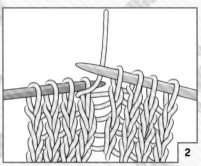

SHORT ROW SHAPING – KNIT SIDE FACING

1. Knit to the last worked stitch. With the yarn held to the back, slip the next stitch purl-wise onto the right needle.

2. Bring the yarn forward, then slip the stitch back to the left needle.

3. Pass yarn to the back. Turn to work in the other direction.

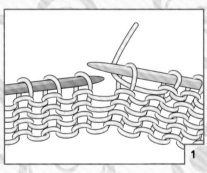

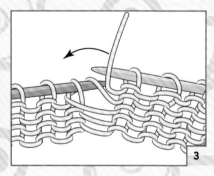

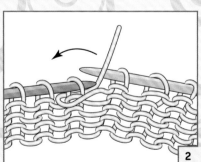

SHORT ROW SHAPING – PURL SIDE FACING

1. Purl to last worked stitch. With yarn held to the back, slip the next stitch purl-wise onto the right needle.

2. Bring the yarn forward, then slip the stitch back to the left needle.

3. Keeping yarn in front, turn and work in the other direction.

SEAMING AND FINISHING

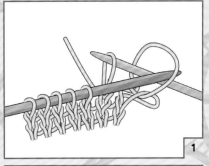

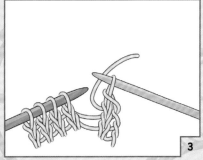

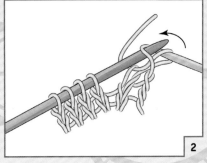

BINDING OFF

1. Complete the next two stitches. Using the tip of the left needle, insert it into the first completed stitch.

2. Lift the loop up and over the second knitted stitch.

3. You should now have only one stitch on the right needle. Pull secure, and knit the next stitch. Repeat until all stitches are bound off. Pull tail of yarn through last stitch and secure.

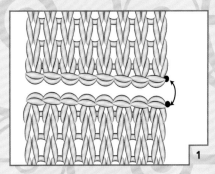

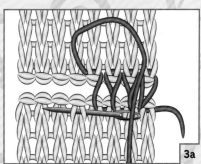

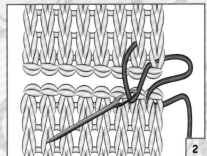

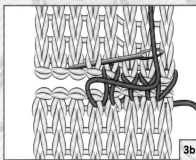

MATTRESS STITCH

1. Line up your knitted edges with right sides facing each other.

2. Using a yarn needle with the same color yarn as the piece, insert the needle from right to left through the first horizontal bar of the lower piece, just below the cast-on stitch. Pull yarn through. Insert the needle from right to left into the first horizontal bar of the upper piece. Pull yarn through.

3. Insert the needle from right to left into the next horizontal bar of the lower piece. Pull yarn through. Insert the needle from right to left into the next horizontal bar of the upper piece. Pull yarn through. Continue alternating in this fashion until the seam is complete. Weave in loose ends.

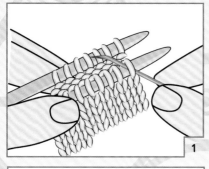

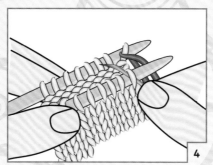

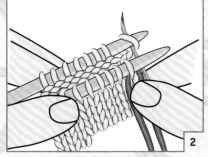

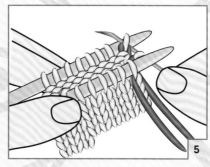

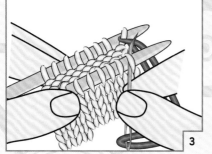

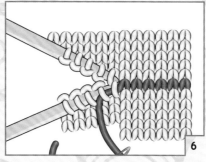

KITCHENER STITCH

1. Holding your needles side-by-side with the wrong sides together, line up the needles and stitches. Place the yarn tail on a yarn needle. Insert the needle purl-wise into the first stitch of the side facing you, and pull the yarn through.

2. Insert the needle knit-wise into the first stitch on the backside and pull the yarn through.

3. Insert the needle into the first stitch in the front knit-wise. Pull the yarn through and pull the stitch off the needle.

4. Insert the needle purl-wise into the first stitch of the side facing you, and pull the yarn through.

5. Insert the needle into the first stitch in the back purl-wise. Pull the yarn through and pull the stitch off the needle.

6. Repeat from Step 2 until all the stitches have been completed. Weave in any loose ends.

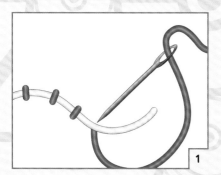

COUCHING

1. Lay the length of embroidery thread (or yarn) along the toy's surface in the desired shape. Using a sewing needle and matching sewing thread, sew into place. Be careful not to pull the sewing thread too tight.

JIGGLYPUFF

OFFICIAL COLORS

NATIONAL POKÉDEX NO.	TYPE	WEIGHT	HEIGHT
0039	Normal/Fairy	12.1 lbs/5.5 kg	1 ft 8 in/0.5 m

When its huge eyes waver, it sings a mysteriously soothing melody that lulls its enemies to sleep.

MATERIALS

- Cascade 220 (100% wool), 10-ply/aran, 100g (220yd/200m), in the following shade:
- Soft pink (4192); 1 ball
- Set of five US size 5 (3.75mm) DPNs
- 12in (30cm) of black yarn or thread for mouth
- Felt pieces in black, white, and green
- Fabric glue
- Polyester filling

GAUGE

22 sts and 24 rows measure 4 x 4in (10 x 10cm) over stockinette stitch (stocking stitch) using US 5 (3.75mm) needles

FINISHED SIZE

6in (15cm) tall

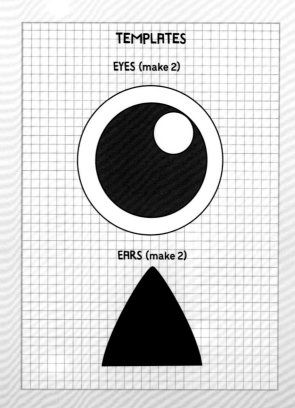

TEMPLATES

EYES (make 2)

EARS (make 2)

BODY (worked from bottom up)

Using US 5 (3.75mm) DPNs, CO 4 sts, split evenly between 4 DPNs, PM, join to knit in the round.

Round 1: [Kfb] 4 times. (8 sts)

Round 2: [Kfb] 8 times. (16 sts)

Round 3: Knit.

Round 4: [K1, m1, k2, m1, k1] 4 times. (24 sts)

Round 5: Knit.

Round 6: [K2, m1, k2, m1, k2] 4 times. (32 sts)

Round 7: Knit.

Round 8: [K3, m1, knit to last 3 sts on needle, m1, k3] 4 times. (40 sts)

Rounds 9–14: Repeat rounds 7–8 three times more, until you have 64 sts, 16 sts on each needle.

Rounds 15–17: Knit.

Round 18: [K3, m1, knit to last 3 sts on needle, m1, k3] 4 times. (72 sts)

Rounds 19–22: Repeat rounds 15–18 once more. (80 sts)

Rounds 23–35: Knit.

Round 36: [K3, k2tog, knit to last 5 sts on needle, k2tog, k3] 4 times. (72 sts)

Rounds 37–39: Knit.

Rounds 40–44: Repeat rounds 36–39 once more. (64 sts)

Round 45: Knit.

Round 46: [K3, k2tog, knit to last 5 sts on needle, k2tog, k3] 4 times. (56 sts)

Rounds 47–56: Repeat rounds 40–41 three times more. (32 sts)

Stuff the body until it is almost fully stuffed.

Round 57: [K2, k2tog, k2tog, k2] 4 times. (24 sts)

Round 58: Knit.

Round 59: [K1, k2tog, k2tog, k1] 4 times. (16 sts)

Stuff rest of body.

Round 60: [K2tog] 8 times. (8 sts)

Round 61: [K2tog] 4 times. (4 sts)

Break yarn, weave loose end through remaining stitches, knot, pull knot to inside of fabric to secure.

FEET (make 2)

Using US 5 (3.75mm) DPNs, CO 5 sts, PM, join to knit in the round.

Round 1: [Kfb] 5 times. (10 sts)

Round 2: Knit.

Round 3: [K1, kfb, k1, kfb, k1] twice. (14 sts)

Rounds 4–13: Knit 10 rounds. Lightly stuff CO end of foot.

Round 14: [K2tog] 7 times.

Break yarn leaving long tail for sewing, weave loose end through remaining stitches, knot, pull knot to inside of fabric to secure.

BODY

FEET

PROJECT 01 / JIGGLYPUFF

ARMS (make 2)

Using US 5 (3.75mm) DPNs, CO 10 sts, PM, join to knit in the round.

Rounds 1–5: Knit 5 rounds.

Round 6: [K2tog] 5 times. (5 sts)

Break yarn leaving long tail for sewing, weave loose end through remaining stitches, knot, pull knot to inside of fabric to secure.

EARS (make 2)

Using US 5 (3.75mm) DPNs, CO 22 sts, PM, join to knit in the round.

Rounds 1–2: Knit.

Round 3: [K1, k2tog, k5, k2tog, k1] twice. (18 sts)

Round 4: Knit.

Round 5: [K1, k2tog, k3, k2tog, k1] twice. (14 sts)

Round 6: Knit.

Round 7: [K1, k2tog, k1, k2tog, k1] twice. (10 sts)

Round 8: Knit.

Round 9: [K2tog, k1, k2tog] twice. (6 sts)

Round 10: Knit.

Round 11: [K2tog] 3 times. (3 sts)

Break yarn, weave loose end through remaining stitches, pull tight and weave in loose end.

HAIR TUFT

Using US 5 (3.75mm) DPNs, CO 6 sts, PM, join to knit in the round.

Round 1: [Kfb] 6 times. (12 sts)

Round 2 and all even numbered rounds: Knit.

Round 3: [Kfb, k1] 6 times. (18 sts)

Round 5: [Kfb, k2] 6 times. (24 sts)

Round 7: [Kfb, k3] 6 times. (30 sts)

Rounds 8–12: Work in stockinette st, starting with a purl row.

Round 13: [K2tog, k3] 6 times. (24 sts)

Rounds 14–18: Work in stockinette st, starting with a purl row.

Round 19: [K2tog, k2] 6 times. (18 sts)

Stuff tuft.

Rounds 20–24: Work in stockinette st, starting with a purl row.

Round 25: [K2tog, k1] 6 times. (12 sts)

Rounds 26–28: Work in stockinette st, starting with a purl row.

Add more stuffing.

Round 29: [K2tog] 6 times. (6 sts)

Break yarn leaving a long tail for sewing, weave loose end through remaining stitches, knot, then pull knot to inside of fabric to secure.

Using loose end from BO end, weave tail in and out of the side of the fabric, approximately 1in (2.5cm) upward towards CO end. Pull tight to curl end of hair tuft upward into itself. Knot well to secure. Pull knot to inside of fabric.

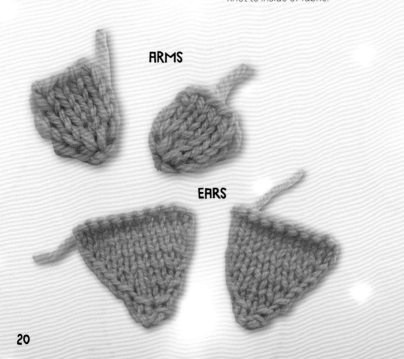

ARMS

EARS

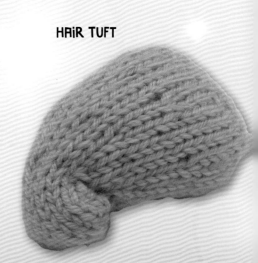

HAIR TUFT

ASSEMBLY

Cut out all felt pieces using templates.

Use images as guides for positioning.

Glue felt pieces for eyes and ears.

Using black yarn or embroidery floss, sew a 1in (2.5cm) line across center of face in the shape of a small smile.

Sew ears to sides of head.

Sew hair tuft to head, centering larger end between ears, and with the curl in front tilted slightly to the side.

Sew legs to bottom of body.

Sew arms to body.

Be sure to weave in all ends to ensure a smooth finish.

PiKACHU

OFFICIAL COLORS

NATIONAL POKÉDEX NO.	TYPE	WEIGHT	HEIGHT
0025	Electric	13.2 lbs/ 6.0 kg	1 ft 4 in/ 0.4 m

When it is angered, it immediately discharges the energy stored in the pouches in its cheeks.

MATERIALS

- Cascade 220 (100% wool), 10-ply/ aran, 100g (220yd/200m), in the following shades:
- Neon yellow (7828); 100yd/92m (**A**)
- Brown (8686); 25yd/23m (**B**)
- Black (8555); 25yd/23m (**C**)
- Set of five size US 5 (3.75mm) DPNs
- Felt pieces in black, brown, white, and red
- Fabric glue
- Polyester filling

GAUGE

22 sts and 26 rows measure 4 x 4in (10 x 10cm) over stockinette stitch (stocking stitch) using US 5 (3.75mm) needles

FINISHED SIZE

6½in (17cm) tall

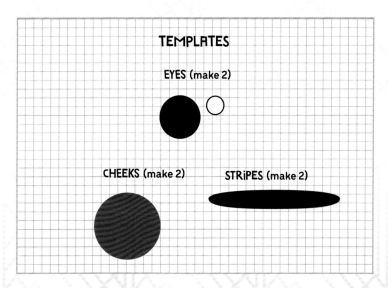

TEMPLATES

EYES (make 2)

CHEEKS (make 2)

STRIPES (make 2)

BODY (worked from bottom up)

Using US 5 (3.75mm) DPNs and **A**, CO 4 sts, split evenly between 4 DPNs, PM, join to knit in the round.

Round 1: [Kfb] 4 times. (8 sts)

Round 2: [Kfb] 8 times. (16 sts)

Round 3: Knit.

Round 4: [K1, m1, k2, m1, k1] 4 times. (24 sts)

Round 5: Knit.

Round 6: [K2, m1, k2, m1, k2] 4 times. (32 sts)

Round 7: Knit.

Round 8: [K3, m1, knit to last 3 sts on needle, m1, k3] 4 times. (40 sts)

Rounds 9–12: Repeat rounds 7 and 8 twice more. (56 sts)

Round 13: Knit.

Round 14: K17, m1, k10, m1, k29. (58 sts)

Rounds 15–23: Knit.

Round 24: K18, k2tog, k6, k2tog, k30. (56 sts)

Rounds 25–27: Knit.

Round 28: [K18, k2tog, k4, k2tog, k2] twice. (52 sts)

Rounds 29–31: Knit.

Round 32: [K4, k2tog, k4, k2tog, k6, k2tog, k2, k2tog, k2] twice. (44 sts)

Round 33: Knit.

Round 34: K8, kfb, k5, kfb, k3, kfb, k5, kfb, k11, kfb, k3, kfb, k3. (50 sts)

Round 35: K9, kfb, k17, kfb, knit to end. (52 sts)

Round 36: K10, kfb, k17, kfb, knit to end. (54 sts)

Round 37: K11, kfb, k8, m1, k2, m1, k7, kfb, knit to end. (58 sts)

Round 38: K12, kfb, k9, m1, k2, m1, k8, kfb, knit to end. (62 sts)

Round 39: Knit.

Round 40: K24, k2tog, ssk, knit to end. (60 sts)

Round 41: K12, k2tog, k8, k2tog, ssk, k8, k2tog, knit to end. (56 sts)

Round 42: K20, k2tog, ssk, knit to end. (54 sts)

Round 43: Knit.

Round 44: K11, k2tog, k16, k2tog, knit to end. (52 sts)

Round 45: Knit.

Round 46: K10, k2tog, k16, k2tog, knit to end. (50 sts)

Round 47: Knit.

Round 48: K9, k2tog, k16, k2tog, knit to end. (48 sts)

Rounds 49–52: Knit.

Round 53: [K3, k2tog, k2, k2tog, k3] 4 times. (40 sts)

Round 54: Knit.

Stuff body.

Round 55: [K2, k2tog, k2, k2tog, k2] 4 times. (32 sts)

Round 56: Knit.

Round 57: [K1, k2tog, k2, k2tog, k1] 4 times. (24 sts)

Round 58: Knit.

Round 59: [K1, k2tog, k2tog, k1] 4 times. (16 sts)

Round 60: Knit.

Stuff remainder of body.

Round 61: [K2tog] 8 times. (8 sts)

Round 62: [K2tog] 4 times. (4 sts)

Break yarn. Use yarn needle to thread tail through remaining sts. Stuff remaining space through opening. Pull tight, knot, pull knot to inside of fabric.

EARS (make 2)

Using US 5 (3.75mm) DPNs and **A**, CO 5 sts, PM, join to knit in the round. Leave a 3–4in (8–10cm) tail for seaming.

Round 1: [Kfb] 5 times. (10 sts)

Round 2: Knit.

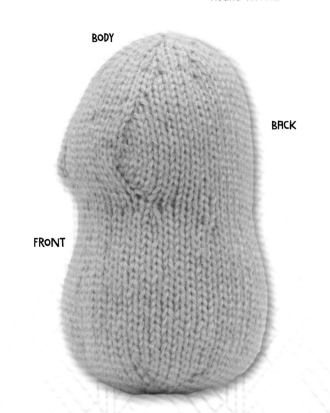

BODY

BACK

FRONT

EARS

Round 3: [Kfb, k4] twice. (12 sts)

Rounds 4–9: Knit.

Stranding yarn not in use loosely across the wrong side, join colors as needed and work pattern as follows.

Round 10: K5 in **A**, k2 in **C**, k5 in **A**.

Round 11: K4 in **A**, k4 in **C**, k4 in **A**.

Round 12: K3 in **A**, k6 in **C**, k3 in **A**.

Round 13: K2 in **A**, k8 in **C**, k2 in **A**.

Round 14: K1 in **A**, k10 in **C**, k1 in **A**.

Break **A**. Continue in **C** only.

Round 15: [K1, k2tog, k3] twice. (10 sts)

Stuff ear.

Round 16: Knit,

Round 17: [K2tog, k3] twice. (8 sts)

Round 18: Knit.

Round 19: [K2tog] 4 times. (4 sts)

Break yarn. Use yarn needle to thread tail through remaining sts. Stuff remaining space through opening. Pull tight, knot, pull knot to inside of fabric.

FEET (make 2)

Using US 5 (3.75mm) DPNs and **A**, CO 4 sts, PM, join to knit in the round. Leave a 3–4in (8–10cm) tail for seaming.

Round 1: [Kfb] 4 times. (8 sts)

Rounds 2–8: Knit.

Stuff foot.

Round 9: [K2tog] 4 times. (4 sts)

Break yarn, pull tail through remaining sts. Stuff remaining space through opening. Pull tight, knot, pull knot to inside of fabric.

ARMS (make 2)

Using US 5 (3.75mm) DPNs and **A**, CO 5 sts, PM, join to knit in the round.

Round 1: [Kfb] 5 times. (10 sts)

Rounds 2–11: Knit.

Stuff arm.

Round 12: [K2tog] 5 times. (5 sts)

Break yarn leaving long tail. Use yarn needle to thread tail through remaining sts.

TRiL (worked top down)

Using US 5 (3.75mm) DPNs and **A**, CO 44 sts, PM, join to knit in the round.

Rounds 1–2: Knit.

Round 3: [K1, k2tog, k16, k2tog, k1] twice. (40 sts)

Rounds 4–5: Knit.

Round 6: [K1, k2tog, k14, k2tog, k1] twice. (36 sts)

Rounds 7–8: Knit.

Round 9: [K1, k2tog, k12, k2tog, k1] twice. (32 sts)

Rounds 10–11: Knit.

Round 12: K6, BO 20 sts, k6. (12 sts).

Round 13: Knit.

Round 14: K1, k2tog, k2, m1, k2, m1, k2, k2tog, k1.

Round 15–16: Knit.

Round 17: K1, k2tog, k2, m1, k2, m1, k2, k2tog, k1.

Round 18: Knit.

Round 19: K12, remove marker, CO 7 sts, PM, CO 7 sts, knit to end of round. (26 sts)

Round 20: Knit.

Round 21: K1, k2tog, k9, m1, k2, m1, k9, k2tog, k1.

Rounds 22–23: Knit.

Round 24: K4, BO 18 sts, k4. (8 sts)

Round 25: K1, k2tog, m1, k2, m1, k2tog, k1.

Round 26: [K1 in **A**, k1 in **B**] 4 times. Break **A**.

Round 27: Knit in **B**.

Round 28: CO 8 sts, k8. (16 sts)

Rounds 29–30: Knit.

Round 31: K8, BO 8 sts. (8 sts)

Round 32: K4, CO 4 sts, k4. (12 sts)

Rounds 33–34: Knit 2 rounds.

BO.

Seam closed all BO and CO edges, stuffing lightly as you go.

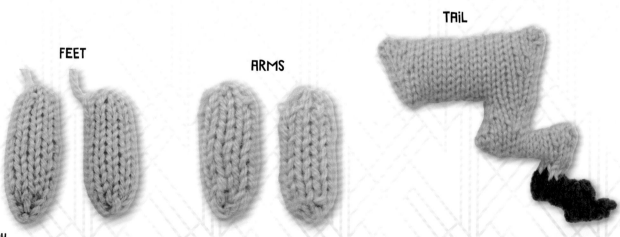

FEET   ARMS   TRiL

ASSEMBLY

Cut out all felt pieces using templates.

Use images as guides for positioning.

Glue felt pieces to face.

Use **C** to create nose and mouth.

Glue brown felt strips to back.

Sew ears to body.

Sew tail to body at base of back. Tack top of tail to base of head.

Sew arms to body.

Sew legs to body.

Be sure to weave in all ends to ensure a smooth finish.

PSYDUCK

OFFICIAL COLORS

NATIONAL POKÉDEX NO.	TYPE	WEIGHT	HEIGHT
0054	Water	43.2 lbs/ 19.6 kg	2 ft 7 in/ 0.8 m

Poor Psyduck suffers from relentless headaches. When the headache turns intense, it begins using mysterious powers.

MATERIALS

- Cascade 220 (100% wool), 10 to ply/aran, 100g (220yd/200m), in the following shades:

- Gold fusion (9669); 1 ball (**A**)

- Butter (8687); 1 ball (**B**)

- Black (8555); 1 ball (**C**)

- Set of five US size 5 (3.75mm) DPNs

- Felt pieces in white and black

- Fabric glue

- Polyester filling

GAUGE

20 sts and 24 rows measure 4 x 4in (10 x 10cm) over stockinette stitch (stocking stitch) using US 5 (3.75mm) needles

FINISHED SIZE

7in (18cm) tall

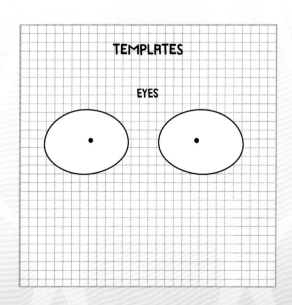

TEMPLATES

EYES

BODY

Using US 5 (3.75mm) DPNs and **A**, CO 4 sts, PM, join to knit in the round.

Round 1: [Kfb] 4 times. (8 sts)

Round 2: [Kfb] 8 times. (16 sts)

Divide sts evenly between 4 DPNs, 4 sts per needle.

Round 3: Knit.

Round 4: [K1, m1, k2, m1, k1] 4 times. (24 sts)

Round 5: Knit.

Round 6: [K2, m1, k2, m1, k2] 4 times. (32 sts)

Round 7: Knit.

Round 8: [K3, m1, knit to last 3 sts on current needle, m1, k3] 4 times. (40 sts)

Rounds 9–14: Repeat rounds 7–8 three times more, until you have 64 sts, 16 on each needle.

Rounds 15–17: Knit.

Round 18: [K3, m1, knit to last 3 sts on current needle, m1, k3] 4 times. (72 sts)

Rounds 19–35: Knit.

Round 36: [K3, k2tog, knit to last 5 sts on current needle, k2tog, k3] 4 times. (64 sts)

Rounds 37–39: Knit.

Round 41: [K3, k2tog, knit to last 5 sts on current needle, k2tog, k3] 4 times. (56 sts)

Round 42: Knit.

Rounds 43–48: Repeat rounds 41–42 three times more. (32 sts, 8 on each needle)

Stuff the body until almost full.

Round 49: [K2, k2tog, k2tog, k2] 4 times. (24 sts)

Round 50: Knit.

Round 51: [K1, k2tog, k2tog, k1] 4 times. (16 sts)

Stuff remaining body.

Round 53: [K2tog] 8 times. (8 sts)

Round 54: [K2tog] 4 times. (4 sts)

Break yarn, weave loose end through remaining sts, knot, pull knot to inside of fabric to secure.

HEAD

Using US 5 (3.75mm) DPNs and **A**, CO 4 sts, PM, join to knit in the round.

Round 1: [Kfb] 4 times. (8 sts)

Round 2: [Kfb] 8 times. (16 sts)

Divide sts evenly between 4 DPNs, 4 sts per needle.

Round 3: Knit.

Round 4: [K1, m1, k2, m1, k1] 4 times. (24 sts)

Round 5: Knit.

Round 6: [K2, m1, k2, m1, k2] 4 times. (32 sts)

Round 7: Knit.

Round 8: [K3, m1, knit to last 3 sts on current needle, m1, k3] 4 times. (40 sts)

Rounds 9–10: Repeat rounds 7–8 one more time, until you have 48 sts, 12 on each needle.

Rounds 11–13: Knit.

Round 14: [K3, m1, knit to last 3 sts on current needle, m1, k3] 4 times. (56 sts)

Rounds 15–30: Knit.

Round 31: [K3, k2tog, knit to last 5 sts on current needle, k2tog, k3] 4 times. (48 sts)

Rounds 32–34: Knit.

BO. Stuff head.

ARMS (make 2)

Using US 5 (3.75mm) DPNs and **A**, CO 5 sts.

Row 1: Kfb, k2, kfb, k1. (7 sts)

Row 2: Purl.

Row 3: K1, m1, knit to last st, m1, k1. (9 sts)

Rows 4–7: Repeat rows 2 and 3 until you have 13 sts.

Row 8: Purl.

Row 9: K13, CO 7 sts. (20 sts)

PM, join to knit in the round.

Rounds 10–13: Knit.

Round 14: K1, k2tog, k7, k2tog, knit to end. (18 sts)

Rounds 15–17: Knit.

Round 18: K2tog, k7, k2tog, knit to end. (16 sts)

Rounds 19–21: Knit.

Round 22: [K2tog, k4, k2tog] twice. (12 sts)

Round 23: Knit.

Divide for fingers: Divide sts evenly between 2 DPNs, 6 on each needle.

Round 24: K2tog, leave next 8 sts on DPNs, knit together the last 2 sts.

Break yarn, pull tail through first and last st to make first finger.

Reattach working yarn to next st.

Round 25: K2tog, leave next 4 sts on DPNs, knit together the last 2 sts.

Break yarn, pull tail through first and last st to make middle finger. Reattach working yarn to next st.

Round 26: [K2tog] twice.

Break yarn, pull tail through remaining sts to make last finger.

Weave in loose ends. Stuff arm.

BODY

HEAD

ARMS

PROJECT 03 / PSYDUCK

BEAK

Using US 5 (3.75mm) DPNs and **B**, CO 4 sts, PM, join to knit in the round.

Round 1: [Kfb] 4 times. (8 sts)

Round 2: [Kfb] 8 times. (16 sts)

Round 3: Knit.

Round 4: [K1, m1, k2, m1, k2, m1, k2, m1, k1] twice. (24 sts)

Round 5: Knit.

Round 6: [K4, m1, k4, m1, k4] twice. (28 sts)

Round 7: Knit.

Round 8: [K4, m1, k6, m1, k4] twice. (32 sts)

Round 9: Knit.

Round 10: [K4, m1, k8, m1, k4] twice. (36 sts)

Rounds 11–18: Knit.

Round 19: [K1, k2tog, k12, k2tog, k1] twice. (32 sts)

Rounds 20–25: Knit.

Round 26: [K2, m1, k12, m1, k2] twice. (36 sts)

Round 27: Knit.

Round 28: K7, m1, k4, m1, knit to end. (38 sts)

Round 29: Knit.

Round 30: K7, m1, k6, m1, knit to end. (40 sts)

BO. Leave long tail for seaming. Stuff lightly.

FEET (make 2)

Using US 5 (3.75mm) DPNs and **B**, CO 6 sts, split evenly between 2 DPNs, join to knit in the round.

Round 1: Knit.

Round 2: [K1, m1, k1, m1, k1] twice. (10 sts)

Rounds 3–5: Knit.

Round 6: [K1, m1, k3, m1, k1] twice. (14 sts)

Rounds 7–9: Knit.

Round 10: [K1, m1, k5, m1, k1] twice. (18 sts)

Rounds 11–15: Knit.

Stuff lightly.

Create toes

Holding 2 DPNs parallel and with yarn attached to first st from the right on back needle, *****k3tog from front needle, then p3tog from back needle. Break yarn, weave loose end through the 2 sts on right needle, knot, and weave to inside of fabric. Reattach yarn to new first st from the right on back needle and repeat from ***** twice more.

TAIL

Using US 5 (3.75mm) DPNs and **A**, CO 7 sts.

Row 1: Kfb, knit to last st, kfb. (9 sts)

Row 2: Pfb, purl to last st, pfb. (11 sts).

Rows 3–6: Repeat rows 1–2 until you have 19 sts.

Row 7: Repeat row 1 once more. (21 sts)

PM, join to knit in the round.

Round 8: Knit.

Round 9: K5, k2tog, K7, k2tog, k5. (19 sts)

Round 10: Knit.

Round 11: K4, k2tog, k2tog, k3, k2tog, k2tog, k4. (15 sts)

Round 12: Knit.

Round 13: K3, k2tog, k5, k2tog, k3. (13 sts)

Round 14: Knit.

Round 15: K2, k2tog, k2tog, k1, k2tog, k2tog, k2. (9 sts)

Round 16: [Sl1, k2tog, psso] 3 times. (3 sts)

Break yarn, pull tail through remaining sts. Knot and pull knot to inside fabric to secure. Stuff tail.

HAIR (make 3)

Using US 5 (3.75mm) DPNs and **C**, CO 2 sts, knit a 1in (2.5cm) long i-cord.
BO.

BEAK

FEET

TAIL

ASSEMBLY

Cut out all felt pieces using templates.

Use images as guides for positioning.

Glue eyes to face, just above beak.

Add black felt pupils, or alternatively, create a knot in the center of the eye using **C**.

Sew hair to top of head.

Sew head to body.

Sew arms to sides of body.

Sew feet to bottom of body.

Sew tail to back of body.

Sew beak to lower part of face.

Use **C** to embroider two nostrils on top center of beak.

Be sure to weave in all ends to ensure a smooth finish.

HAIR

SNORLAX

OFFICIAL COLORS

NATIONAL POKÉDEX NO.	TYPE	WEIGHT	HEIGHT
0143	Normal	1,014.1 lbs/ 460.0 kg	6 ft 11 in/ 2.1 m

Its stomach's digestive juices can dissolve any kind of poison. Eating things off the ground doesn't bother it at all.

MATERIALS

- Cascade 220 (100% wool), 10 to ply/aran, 100g (220yd/200m), in the following shades:

- Pacific (2433); 1 ball (**A**)

- Pear (8412); 1 ball (**B**)

- 2yds (1.8m) yards fingering weight white yarn (**C**)

- 1yd (1m) fingering weight black yarn (**D**)

- Set of five US size 5 (3.75mm) DPNs

- Set of five US size 2 (2.75mm) DPNs

- Felt pieces in white and brown

- Fabric glue

- Polyester filling

GAUGE

22 sts and 24 rows measure 4 x 4in (10 x 10cm) over stockinette stitch (stocking stitch) using US 5 (3.75mm) needles

FINISHED SIZE

8in (20cm) tall

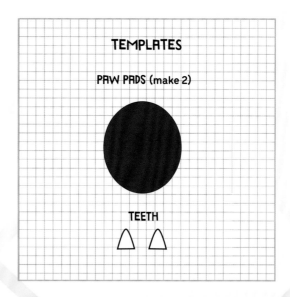

BODY

Using US 5 (3.75mm) DPNs and **A**, CO 8 sts, PM, join to knit in the round.

Round 1: [Kfb] 8 times. (16 sts)

Divide sts evenly over 4 DPNs, 4 sts per needle.

Round 2: Knit.

Round 3: [K1, m1, k2, m1, k1] 4 times. (24 sts)

Round 4: Knit.

Round 5: [K2, m1, k2, m1, k2] 4 times. (32 sts)

Round 6: Knit.

Round 7: [K3, m1, knit to last 3 sts on current needle, m1, k3] 4 times. (40 sts)

Round 8: Knit.

Rounds 9–22: Repeat rounds 7–8 until you have 96 sts, 24 sts on each needle.

Round 23: [K3, m1, k18, m1, k27] twice. (100 sts)

Round 24: Knit.

Round 25: [K3, m1, k20, m1, k27] twice. (104 sts)

Round 26: Knit.

Round 27: [K3, m1, k22, m1, k27] twice. (108 sts)

Rounds 28–45: Knit.

Round 46: [K3, k2tog, k20, k2tog, k27] twice. (104 sts)

Round 47: Knit.

Round 48: [K3, k2tog, k18, k2tog, k27] twice. (100 sts)

Round 49: Knit.

Round 50: [K3, k2tog, k16, k2tog, k27] twice. (96 sts)

Round 51: Knit.

Round 52: [K3, k2tog, knit to last 5 sts on current needle, k2tog, k3] 4 times. (88 sts)

Round 53: Knit.

Rounds 54–63: Repeat rounds 52–53 till you have 48 sts, 12 on each needle.

Round 64: [K3, m1, knit to last 3 sts on current needle, m1, k1] 4 times. (56 sts)

Round 65: Knit.

Rounds 66–69: Repeat round 64–65 twice more. (72 sts)

Rounds 70–77: Knit.

Stuff body.

Round 78: [K3, k2tog, knit to last 5 sts on current needle, k2tog, k3] 4 times. (64 sts)

Round 79: Knit.

Rounds 80 onward: Repeat rounds 78–79 until you have 24 sts remaining, 6 sts on each needle, pausing halfway through to stuff head.

Next round: [K2tog] 12 times. (12 sts)

Next round: [K2tog] 6 times. (6 sts)

Break yarn, pull tail through remaining sts. Stuff head completely, then pull sts tight, knot, and pull knot to inside of fabric. Weave in loose ends.

BODY

PROJECT 04 / SNORLAX

FACE AND BELLY

Using US 5 (3.75mm) DPNs and **B**, CO 12 sts.

Row 1: Kfb, knit to last 2 sts, kfb, k1. (14 sts)

Row 2: P1, m1, purl to last st, m1, p1. (16 sts)

Row 3: K1, m1, knit to last st, m1, k1. (18 sts)

Rows 4–7: Repeat rows 2–3 twice more. (26 sts)

Row 8: Purl.

Row 9: K1, m1, knit to last st, m1, k1. (28 sts)

Rows 10–16: Work in stockinette st.

Row 17: K1, k2tog, knit to last 3 sts, k2tog, k1. (26 sts)

Row 18: Purl.

Rows 19–30: Repeat rows 17–18 until 14 sts remain.

Row 31: K1, m1, knit to last st, m1, k1. (16 sts)

Row 32: Purl.

Rows 33–34: Repeat rows 31–32. (18 sts)

Rows 35–38: Work in stockinette st.

Row 39: K1, k2tog, knit to last 3 sts, k2tog, k1. (16 sts)

Row 40: Purl.

Rows 41 onward: Repeat rows 39–40 until 12 sts remain.

Split for eyes

*****Next row:** K2tog, k2, k2tog, turn. Leave last 6 sts on a separate dpn. (4 sts)

Next row: Purl.

Next row: K2tog twice. (2 sts)

Break yarn, weave through remaining sts, knot, weave tail into purl side of fabric.

Reattach working yarn to next st and repeat from *****.

Lightly press.

EARS (make 2)

Using US 5 (3.75mm) DPNs and **A**, and long tail cast on, CO 20 sts, split evenly between two DPNs, 10 sts on each needle, PM, join to knit in the round. Leave a long tail for seaming ear to head.

Round 1: Knit.

Round 2: [K1, k2tog, knit to last 3 sts on current needle, k2tog, k1] twice. (16 sts)

Rounds 3 onward: Repeat rounds 1–2 until you have 8 sts remaining.

Next round: [K2tog] 4 times. (4 sts)

Break yarn, pull tail through remaining sts. Pull sts tight, knot, and pull knot to inside of fabric. Weave in loose ends. Stuff lightly.

ARMS (make 2)

Using US 5 (3.75mm) DPNs and **A**, CO 6 sts, PM, join to knit in the round.

Round 1: [Kfb] 6 times. (12 sts)

Round 2: [Kfb, k1] 6 times. (18 sts)

Round 3: Knit.

Round 4: [Kfb, k2] 6 times. (24 sts)

Rounds 5 onward: Work in stockinette st until arm measures 3in (8cm).

BO leaving a 10in (25cm) tail for seaming. Stuff arms.

CLAWS (make 10)

Using US 2 (2.75mm) DPNs and **C**, CO 2 sts. Knit 4 rounds of i-cord. BO.

FEET (make 2)

Using US 5 (3.75mm) DPNs and **B**, CO 5 sts.

Row 1: Kfb, k2, kfb, k1. (7 sts)

Row 2: Purl.

Row 3: K1, m1, knit to last 2 sts, m1, k1. (9 sts)

Rows 4–7: Repeat rows 2–3 twice more. (13 sts)

Rows 8–14: Work in stockinette st.

Row 15: K1, k2tog, knit to last 3 sts, k2tog, k1. (11 sts)

Row 16: Purl.

Rows 17 onward: Repeat rows 15–16 until 7 sts remain.

Next row: Bind off as you complete this row, k1, k2tog, k1, k2tog, k1.

TOP OF RIGHT FOOT

Place foot knit side up. Imagine the foot is a clock face, begin picking up sts at about 4 o'clock. Using US 5 (3.75mm) DPNs and **B**, join to knit in the round.

Round 1: Knit.

Round 2: K10, k2tog, k3, k2tog, k19. (34 sts)

Round 3: K26, w&t.

Round 4: P9, p2tog, p3, p2tog, p2, w&t. (32 sts)

Round 5: K12, w&t.

Round 6: P8, w&t.

Round 7: Knit to end.

BO. Stuff foot.

FACE AND BELLY

EARS

ARMS AND CLAWS

TOP OF LEFT FOOT

Place foot knit side up. Imagine the foot is a clock face, begin picking up sts at about 8 o'clock. Using US 5 (3.75mm) DPNs and **B**, pick up and knit 36 sts around edge of foot, PM, join to knit in the round.

Round 1: Knit.

Round 2: K19, k2tog, k3, k2tog, k10. (34 sts)

Round 3: K26, w&t.

Round 4: P2, p2tog, p3, p2tog, p9, w&t. (32 sts)

Round 5: K12, w&t.

Round 6: P8, w&t.

Round 7: Knit to end.

BO. Stuff foot.

FOOT CLAWS (make 6)

Using US 2 (2.75mm) DPNs and **C**, CO 12 sts, PM, join to knit in the round.

Round 1: Knit.

Round 2: [K2tog] 6 times. (6 sts)

Round 3: Knit.

Round 4: [K2tog] 3 times. (3 sts).

Break yarn, pull tail through remaining sts. Pull sts tight, knot, and pull knot to inside of fabric.

ASSEMBLY

Cut out all felt pieces using templates.

Use images as guides for positioning.

Sew ears to top of head.

Sew claws to ends of arms in a straight row of five on each arm. Fold and sew other end of each claw to hand.

Sew claws to tips of feet.

Sew feet to bottom of body.

Sew face and belly to front of body.

Use **D** to create eyes and mouth.

Glue teeth to upper edge of mouth.

Glue paw pads to both feet.

Be sure to weave in all ends to ensure a smooth finish.

LEFT FOOT   **RIGHT FOOT**

GENGAR

OFFICIAL COLORS

NATIONAL POKÉDEX NO.	TYPE	WEIGHT	HEIGHT
0094	Ghost/ Poison	89.3 lbs/ 40.5 kg	4 ft 11 in/ 1.5 m

Hiding in people's shadows at night, it absorbs their heat. The chill it causes makes the victims shake.

MATERIALS

- Cascade 220 (100% wool), 10-ply/ aran, 100g (220yd/200m), in the following shades:

- Purple hyacinth (7808); 1 ball (**A**)

- Black (8555); 20yd/18m (**B**)

- Set of five size US size 5 (3.75mm) DPNs

- Felt pieces in black, white, and red

- Fabric glue

- Polyester filling

GAUGE

22 sts and 26 rows measure 4 x 4in (10 x 10cm) over stockinette stitch (stocking stitch) using US 5 (3.75mm) needles

FINISHED SIZE

8½in (21cm) tall

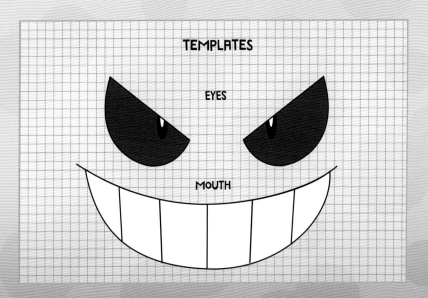

TEMPLATES

EYES

MOUTH

BODY (worked from top down)

Using US 5 (3.75mm) DPNs and **A**, CO 8 sts, PM, join to knit in the round.

Round 1: [Kfb] 8 times. (16 sts)

Divide sts evenly between 4 DPNs, 4 sts per needle.

Round 2 and all even numbered rounds: Knit.

Round 3: [K1, m1, k2, m1, k1] 4 times. (24 sts)

Round 5: [K2, m1, k2, m1, k2] 4 times. (32 sts)

Round 7: [K3, m1, knit to last 3 sts on current needle, m1, k3] 4 times. (40 sts)

Round 8: Knit.

Round 9–22: Repeat rounds 7–8 until you have 96 sts, 24 on each needle.

Rounds 23–52: Knit.

Round 53: [K3, k2tog, knit to last 5 sts on current needle, k2tog, k3] 4 times. (88 sts)

Round 54: Knit.

Rounds 55–64: Repeat rounds 53–54 until you have 48 sts, 12 on each needle.

Stuff body until almost full.

Round 65: [K3, k2tog, k2, k2tog, k3] 4 times. (40 sts)

Round 67: [K2, k2tog, k2, k2tog, k2] 4 times. (32 sts)

Round 69: [K1, k2tog, k2, k2tog, k1] 4 times. (24 sts)

Round 71: [K1, k2tog, k2tog, k1] 4 times. (16 sts)

Completely stuff body.

Round 73: [K2tog] 8 times. (8 sts)

Round 74: [K2tog] 4 times. (4 sts)

Break yarn, weave loose end through remaining sts, knot, pull knot to inside of fabric.

FEET (make 2)

Using US 5 (3.75mm) DPNs and A, cast on 6 sts, PM, join to knit in the round. Split sts evenly between 2 needles, 3 sts on each needle.

Round 1: Knit.

Round 2: [K1, m1, k1, m1, k1] twice. (10 sts)

Round 3: Knit.

Round 4: [K1, m1, k3, m1, k1] twice. (14 sts)

Round 5: Knit.

Round 6: [K1, m1, k5, m1, k1] twice. (18 sts)

Round 7: Knit.

Round 8: [K1, m1, k7, m1, k1] twice. (22 sts)

Rounds 9–13: Knit.

Round 14: [K1, k2tog, k5, k2tog, k1] twice. (18 sts)

Round 15: Knit.

Create toes

Holding 2 DPNs parallel and with yarn attached to first st from the right on back needle, *k3tog from front needle, then p3tog from back needle. Break yarn, weave loose end through the 2 sts on right needle, knot, and weave to inside of fabric. Reattach yarn to new first st from the right on back needle and repeat from * twice more.

LEGS (make 2)

Using US 5 (3.75mm) DPNs and **A**, cast on 24 sts, PM, join to knit in the round.

Rounds 1–5: Knit.

Round 6: [K1, m1, k4, m1, k1] 4 times. (32 sts)

Rounds 7–10: Knit.

Round 11: [BO 8, knit to last 2 sts, k2tog]. (23 sts)

Continue knitting in rows.

Row 12: [Purl to last 2 sts, p2tog]. (22 sts)

Row 13: [Knit to last 2 sts, k2tog]. (21 sts)

Rows 14–23: Repeat rows 12 and 13 five more times, until 11 sts remain.

Row 24: Repeat row 12 once more. (10 sts)

Row 25: K1, k2tog, k4, k2tog, k1. (8 sts)

Row 26: Purl.

BO, leaving long tail for seaming.

TAIL

Using US 5 (3.75mm) DPNs and **A**, cast on 2 sts, PM, join to knit in the round.

Round 1: [Kfb] twice. (4 sts)

Round 2: [Kfb] 4 times. (8 sts)

Rounds 3–4: Knit.

Round 5: [Kfb] 8 times. (16 sts)

Rounds 6–8: Knit.

Round 9: [K1, m1, k2, m1, k1] 4 times. (24 sts)

Rounds 10–12: Knit.

Round 13: [K2, m1, k2, m1, k2] 4 times. (32 sts)

Rounds 14–16: Knit.

Round 17: [K3, m1, k2, m1, k3] 4 times. (40 sts)

Rounds 18–20: Knit.

BODY

FEET AND LEGS

TAIL

Round 21: BO 10, k to end. (30 sts)
Continue knitting in rows.

Row 22: P2tog, purl to last 2 sts, p2tog. (28 sts)

Row 23: K2tog, knit to last 2 sts, k2tog. (26 sts)

Rows 24 onward: Repeat rounds 22 and 23 four more times until 10 sts remain.

BO. Stuff tail.

ARMS (make 2)

Using US 5 (3.75mm) DPNs and **A**, cast on 9 sts.

Row 1: Kfb, k6, kfb, k1. (11 sts)

Row 2: Purl.

Row 3: K1, m1, knit to last st, m1, k1. (13 sts)

Rows 4–9: Repeat rows 2 and 3 three more times until you have 19 sts.

Row 10: Purl.

Row 11: K19, CO 9. (28 sts)
PM, join to knit in the round.

Rounds 12–14: Knit.

Round 15: K1, k2tog, k13, k2tog, knit to end. (26 sts)

Round 16–18: Knit.

Round 19: K1, k2tog, k11, k2tog, knit to end. (24 sts)

Round 20: Knit.

Round 21: K1, k2tog, k9, k2tog, knit to end. (22 sts)

Round 22: Knit.

Round 23: Sl1, k2tog, k7, k2tog, k2tog, k7, knit last st together with first slipped st. (18 sts)

Round 24: Knit.

Round 25: [K2tog, k2, k2tog, k1, k2tog] twice. (12 sts)

Round 26: Knit.

Divide for fingers: Split sts evenly between 2 DPNs, 6 on each needle.

Next round: K2tog, leave next 8 sts on DPNs or scrap yarn, k2tog. (2 sts)

Break yarn, pull tail through first and last st to make first finger.

Reattach working yarn.

Next round: K2tog, leave next 4 sts on DPNs or scrap yarn, k2tog. (2 sts)

Break yarn, pull tail through first and last st to make middle finger.

Reattach working yarn.

Next round: [K2tog] twice. (2 sts)

Break yarn, pull tail through remaining sts to make last finger.

Weave in loose ends. Stuff arm.

SMALL SPIKE (make 8)

Using US 5 (3.75mm) DPNs and **A**, cast on 12 sts, PM, join to knit in the round.

Rounds 1 and 2: Knit.

Round 3: [K2tog] 6 times. (6 sts)

Round 4: [K2tog] 3 times. (3 sts)

Break yarn, weave loose end through remaining sts, knot, pull knot to inside of fabric. Stuff spikes.

MEDIUM SPIKE (make 7)

Using US 5 (3.75mm) DPNs and **A**, cast on 18 sts, PM, join to knit in the round.

Rounds 1–2: Knit.

Round 3: [K1, k2tog, k2tog, k1] 3 times. (12 sts)

Rounds 5–6: Knit.

Round 7: [K2tog] 6 times. (6 sts)

Round 8: [K2tog] 3 times. (3 sts)

Break yarn, weave loose end through remaining sts, knot, pull knot to inside of fabric. Stuff spikes.

LARGE SPIKE

Using US 5 (3.75mm) DPNs and **A**, cast on 24 sts, PM, join to knit in the round.

Rounds 1–2: Knit.

Round 3: [K1, k2tog, k2, k2tog, k1] 3 times. (18 sts)

Rounds 5–6: Knit.

Round 7: [K1, k2tog, k2tog, k1] 3 times. (12 sts)

Round 8: [K2tog] 6 times. (6 sts)

Round 9: [K2tog] 3 times. (3 sts)

Break yarn, weave loose end through remaining sts, knot, pull knot to inside of fabric. Stuff spike.

EARS (make 2)

Using US 5 (3.75mm) DPNs and **A**, cast on 24 sts, PM, join to knit in the round.

Divide sts evenly between 2 DPNs.

Rounds 1–2: Knit.

Round 3: [K1, k2tog, knit to last 3 sts on current needle, k2tog, k1] twice. (20 sts)

Rounds 4–12: Repeat rounds 1–3 three more times until 8 sts remain.

Rounds 13–14: Knit 2 rounds.

Round 15: [K2tog] 4 times. (4 sts)

Break yarn, weave loose end through remaining sts, knot, pull knot to inside of fabric. Stuff ears.

ARMS

SMALL SPIKE

MEDIUM SPIKE

LARGE SPIKE

ASSEMBLY

Cut out all felt pieces using templates.

Use images as guides for positioning.

Glue felt pieces for eyes and mouth.

Use **B** to outline teeth as shown.

Use **B** to outline upper edges of eyes.

Sew each foot to smaller end of leg. Stuff leg.

Hold body upright in desired position and position legs. Pin into place.

Sew legs to body.

Center tail so that the longer side lines up along the bottom BO edge of body and pin into place.

Sew to body.

Pin arms into place and seam to sides of body.

Pin ears into place and seam to sides of head.

Sew two small spikes, and one medium spike to head between ears in this order, from left to right: small, medium, small.

Sew one large spike, followed by three medium spikes, and ending with two small spikes down center of back.

On each side of center row of spikes, sew two medium spikes followed by two small spikes.

Be sure to weave in all ends to ensure a smooth finish.

EARS

SQUIRTLE

OFFICIAL COLORS

NATIONAL POKÉDEX NO.	TYPE	WEIGHT	HEIGHT
0007	Water	19.8 lbs/ 9.0 kg	1 ft 8 in/ 0.5 m

After birth, its back swells and hardens into a shell. It sprays a potent foam from its mouth.

MATERIALS

- Cascade 220 (100% wool), 10-ply/ aran, 100g (220yd/200m), in the following shades:

- Aqua (8951); 110yd/100m (**A**)

- Jack O Lantern (7824); 110yds/100m (**B**)

- Pear (8412); 110yds/100m (**C**)

- Nimbus Cloud (1058); 55yds/ 50m (**D**)

- Black (8555); 20yds/18m (**E**)

- Set of five size US5 (3.75mm) DPNs

- Felt pieces in black, white, and red

- Fabric glue

- Polyester filling

GAUGE

22 sts and 26 rows measure 4 x 4in (10 x 10cm) over stockinette stitch (stocking stitch) using size US 5 (3.75mm) needles.

FINISHED SIZE

7in (17.8cm) tall

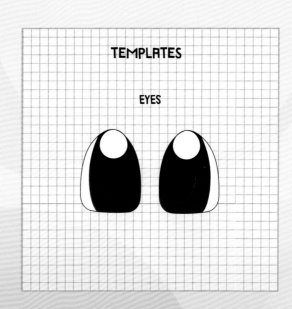

TEMPLATES

EYES

BODY (knit from the bottom up)

Using 3 US5 (3.75mm) DPNs and **C**, CO 8 sts, PM, join to knit in the round.

Round 1: [Kfb] 8 times. (16 sts)

Split sts evenly between 4 DPNs, 4 sts on each needle.

Round 2: Knit.

Round 3: [K1, m1, k2, m1, k1] 4 times. (24 sts)

Round 4: Knit.

Round 5: [K2, m1, knit to last 2 sts on DPN, m1, k2] 4 times. (32 sts)

Repeat rounds 4–5 until you have 56 sts (14 on each DPN)

Rounds 12–25: Knit.

Round 26: [K2, k2tog, knit to last 4 sts on DPN, k2tog, k2] 4 times. (48 sts)

Round 27: Knit.

Repeat rounds 26–27 twice more. (32 sts)

BO. Weave in loose ends. Stuff body.

HEAD (knit from the top down)

Using US5 (3.75mm) DPNs and **A**, CO 4 sts, PM, join to knit in the round.

Round 1: [Kfb] 4 ttimes. (8 sts)

Round 2: [Kfb] 8 times. (16 sts)

Split sts evenly between 4 DPNs, 4 sts on each needle.

Round 3: Knit.

Round 4: [K1, m1, k2, m1, k1] 4 times. (24 sts)

Round 5: Knit.

Round 6: [K2, m1, knit to last 2 sts on DPN, m1, k2] 4 times. (32 sts)

Repeat rounds 5–6 until you have 56 sts (14 on each DPN)

Rounds 13–20: Knit.

Round 21: [K2, k2tog, knit to last 4 sts on DPN, k2tog, k2] 4 times. (48 sts)

Round 22: Knit.

Repeat rounds 21–22 twice more. (32 sts)

BO, leaving a long tail for seaming. Stuff head.

SHELL

Using US5 (3.75mm) DPNs and **B**, CO 4 sts, PM, join to knit in the round.

Round 1: [Kfb] 4 ttimes. (8 sts)

Round 2: [Kfb] 8 times. (16 sts)

Split sts evenly between 4 DPNs, 4 sts on each needle.

Round 3: Knit.

Round 4: [K1, m1, k2, m1, k1] 4 times. (24 sts)

Round 5: Knit.

Round 6: [K2, m1, knit to last 2 sts on DPN, m1, k2] 4 times. (32 sts)

Round 7: Knit.

Round 8: [K3, m1, knit to last 2 sts on DPN, m1, k3] 4 times. (40 sts)

Repeat rounds 7–8 until you have 64 sts (16 on each DPN)

Switch to **D**.

Next round: Knit.

Next round: Purl.

Next round: Knit.

BO purlwise. Weave in loose ends. Press shell lightly.

HEAD

BODY

SHELL

PROJECT 06 / SQUiRTLE

ARMS (make 2)

Using US5 (3.75mm) DPNs and **A**, CO 18 sts, PM, join to knit in the round.

Rounds 1–8: Knit.

Round 9: [K2tog, k1] 6 times. (12 sts)

Round 10: Knit.

Round 11: [K2tog] 6 times. (6 sts)

Break yarn, pull tail through remaining sts.

Fingers

Using **A**, pick up and knit two sts from tip of arm. Knit 1 round of i-cord. BO. Weave in loose ends.

Repeat for an additional finger on each side of center finger, for 3 fingers total in each arm.

LEGS (make 2)

Begin with sole:

Using US5 (3.75mm) DPNs and **A**, CO 6 sts. Work 6 rows in stockinette st.

Create toes

Round 7: : K2tog. Break yarn, pull tail through st just made. Weave loose end into purl side of fabric. Repeat round 7 twice more for remaining 4 sts. Weave in all loose ends.

Using 3.75mm DPNs and **A**, pick up 24 sts around the perimeter of the sole. PM, join to knit in the round.

Knit 10 rounds. BO, leaving long tail for sewing. Stuff leg.

Knit 10 rounds. Bind off, leaving long tail for sewing. Stuff leg.

TAiL

Using US5 (3.75mm) DPNs and **A**, CO 12 sts, PM, join to knit in the round.

Rounds 1–2: Knit.

Round 3: M1, k1, k2tog, k3, k2tog, k1, m1, k3.

Round 4: Knit.

Round 5: M1, k9, m1, k3. (14 sts)

Round 6: Knit.

Round 7: M1, k2, k2tog, k1, m1, k1, m1, k1, k2tog, k2, m1, k1, m1, k1, m1, k1. (18 sts)

Round 8: Knit.

Round 9: M1, k13, m1, k5. (20 sts)

Round 10: Knit.

Round 11: M1, k3, k2tog, k1, m1, k3, m1, k1, k2tog, k3, m1, k1, m1, k3, m1, k1. (24 sts)

Round 12: Knit.

Round 13: M1, k17, m1, k7. (26 sts)

Round 14: M1, k4, k2tog, k1, m1, k5, m1, k1, k2tog, k4, m1, k1, m1, k5, m1, k1. (30 sts)

Round 15: Knit.

Round 16: M1, k5, k2tog, k1, m1, k6, m1, k1, k2tog, k5, m1, k1, m1, k6, m1, k1. (34 sts)

Round 17: Knit.

Round 18: M1, k6, k2tog, k1, m1, k7, m1, k1, k2tog, k6, m1, k1, m1, k7, m1, k1. (38 sts)

Round 19: Knit.

Round 20: M1, k7, k2tog, k1, m1, k8, m1, k1, k2tog, k7, m1, k1, m1, k8, m1, k1. (42 sts)

Rounds 21–25: Knit.

Round 26: K2tog, k5, k2tog, k1, k2tog, k6, k2tog, k1, k2tog, k5, k2tog, k1, k2tog, k6, k2tog, k1. (34 sts)

Round 27: Knit.

Round 28: K2tog, k3, k2tog, k1, k2tog, k4, k2tog, k1, k2tog, k3, k2tog, k1, k2tog, k4, k2tog, k1. (26 sts)

Round 29: Knit.

Round 30: K2tog, k1, k2tog, k1, k2tog, k2, k2tog, k1, k2tog, k1, k2tog, k1, k2tog, k2, k2tog, k1. (18 sts)

Round 31: Knit.

Round 32: [K2tog, k1] 6 times. (12 sts)

Round 33: Knit.

Round 34: [K2tog] 6 times. (6 sts)

Break yarn, pull tail through remaining sts. Weave in loose ends. Stuff tail firmly.

ARMS   LEGS   TAiL

ASSEMBLY

Cut out all felt pieces using templates.

Use images as guides for positioning.

Glue felt pieces for eyes.

Sew head to body.

Wrap shell around body and seam into place.

Sew legs to body.

Sew arms to body.

Use **E** and couching to create patterns on shell, front of body, and swirl in tail.

Use **E** to create mouth, nostrils, and eyebrows.

Be sure to weave in all ends to ensure a smooth finish.

SCORBUNNY

OFFICIAL COLORS

NATIONAL POKÉDEX NO.	TYPE	WEIGHT	HEIGHT
0813	Fire	9.9 lbs/ 4.5 kg	1 ft 0 in/ 0.3 m

Fire energy gathers in the pads of its feet, raising their temperature. Once hot, Scorbunny's footpads can deal heavy damage to opponents.

MATERIALS

- Cascade 220 (100% wool), 10-ply/ aran, 100g (220yd/200m), in the following shades:

- White (8505); 1 ball (**A**)

- Tiger Lily (9605); 110yd/100m (**B**)

- California Poppy (7826); 110yd/100m (**C**)

- Black (8555); Oddments (**D**)

- Orange embroidery thread

- Set of five size US5 (3.75mm) DPNs

- Felt pieces in yellow, black, orange, and white

- Fabric glue

- Polyester filling

GAUGE

22 sts and 26 rows measure 4 x 4in (10 x 10cm) over stockinette stitch (stocking stitch) using size US 5 (3.75mm) needles.

FINISHED SIZE

11in (28cm) tall

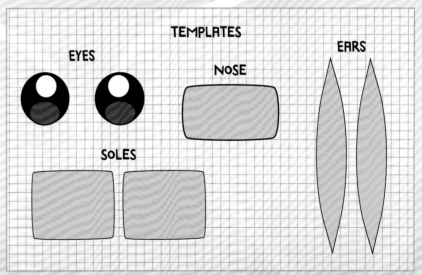

TEMPLATES

EYES

NOSE

EARS

SOLES

BODY (worked from the bottom up)

Using US 5 (3.75mm) DPNs and **A**, CO 4 sts, PM, join to knit in the round.

Round 1: [Kfb] 4 times. (8 sts)

Round 2: [Kfb] 8 times. (16 sts)

Divide sts evenly between 4 DPNs, 4 per needle.

Round 3: Knit.

Round 4: [K1, m1, k2, m1, k1] 4 times. (24 sts)

Round 5: Knit.

Round 6: [K2, m1, k2, m1, k2] 4 times. (32 sts)

Round 7: Knit.

Round 8: [K2, m1, k4, m1, k2] 4 times. (40 sts)

Rounds 9–10: Knit.

Round 11: [K2, k2tog, k2, k2tog, k2] 4 times. (32 sts)

Rounds 12–13: Knit.

Round 14: [K1, k2tog, k2, k2tog, k1] 4 times. (24 sts)

Round 15–16: Knit.

Round 17: [K1, k2tog, k2tog, k1] 4 times. (16 sts)

Round 18: Knit.

BO. Stuff body.

HEAD

Using US 5 (3.75mm) DPNs and **A**, CO 4 sts, PM, join to knit in the round.

Round 1: [Kfb] 4 times. (8 sts)

Round 2: [Kfb] 8 times. (16 sts)

Round 3: Knit.

Round 4: [K1, m1, k2, m1, k1] 4 times. (24 sts)

Round 5: Knit.

Round 6: [K2, m1, k2, m1, k2] 4 times. (32 sts)

Round 7: Knit

Round 8: [K3, m1, knit to last 3 sts on DPN, m1, k3] 4 times. (40 sts)

Repeat rounds 7–8 once more. (56 sts, 14 on each needle

Rounds 11–12: Knit.

Round 13: [K3, m1, knit to last 3 sts on DPN, m1, k3] 4 times. (64 sts)

Rounds 14–18: Knit.

Round 19: [K3, m1, knit to last 3 sts on DPN, m1, k3] 4 times. (64 sts)

Rounds 20–21: Knit.

Round 22: [K3, k2tog, knit to last 5 sts on DPN, k2tog, k3] 4 times. (56 sts)

Round 23: Knit.

Repeat rounds 22–23 three more times. (32 sts, 8 on each needle)

Stuff the head until almost full.

Round 30: [K2, k2tog, k2tog, k2] 4 times. (24 sts)

Round 31: Knit.

Round 32: [K1, k2tog, k2tog, k1] 4 times. (16 sts)

Stuff rest of head.

Round 33: [K2tog] 8 times. (8 sts)

Round 34: [K2tog] 4 times. (4 sts)

Break yarn, pull tail through remaining sts, and pull loose end into inside of fabric.

ARMS (make 2)

Using US 5 (3.75mm) DPNs and **A**, CO 8 sts, PM, join to knit in the round.

Round 1–3: Knit.

Round 4: [K2, m1, k2] twice. (10 sts)

Round 5: Knit.

Round 6: [K1, m1, k3, m1, k1] twice. (14 sts)

Rounds 7–9: Knit.

Round 10: [K1, m1, k5, m1, k1] twice. (18 sts)

Rounds 11–14: Knit.

Round 15: [K1, m1, k7, m1, k1] twice. (22 sts)

Rounds 16–18: Knit.

Round 19: [K1, k2tog, k5, k2tog, k1] twice. (18 sts)

Round 20: [K1, k2tog, k3, k2tog, k1] twice. (14 sts)

Stuff arm. BO with kitchener st.

BODY

HEAD

ARMS

PROJECT 07 / SCORBUNNY

FEET (make 2)

Using US 5 (3.75mm) DPNs and **A**, CO 4 sts, PM, join to knit in the round.

Round 1: [Kfb] 4 times. (8 sts)

Round 2: [K2, kfb, kfb] twice. (12 sts)

Round 3: Knit.

Round 4: [K1, m1, k3, m1, k2] twice. (16 sts)

Rounds 5–6: Knit.

Round 7: [K5, m1, k3] twice. (18 sts)

Rounds 8–10: Knit.

Round 11: [K6, m1, k3] twice. (20 sts)

Rounds 12–14: Knit.

Round 15: [K7, m1, k3] twice. (22 sts)

Rounds 16–19: Knit.

Switch to **B**.

Rounds 20–21: Knit.

Round 22: K2tog, k10, k2tog, knit to end. (20 sts)

Round 23: Knit.

Round 24: [K3, k2tog, k2, k2tog, k1] twice. (16 sts)

Round 25: Knit.

Round 26: S1, k2tog, k4, [k2tog] twice, k4, knit last st together with slipped st from beginning of round. (12 sts)

Stuff foot. Divide sts evenly between 2 DPNs. BO with kitchener st.

LEGS (make 2)

Using US 5 (3.75mm) DPNs and **A**, CO 4 sts.

Knit a 1in (2.5cm) i-cord. BO, leaving a tail for seaming.large

LARGE CHEEK TRIM (make 2)

Using US 5 (3.75mm) DPNs and **A**, CO 4 sts, PM, join to knit in the round.

Round 1: Knit.

Round 2: [K1, m1, k1] twice. (6 sts)

Round 3: Knit.

Round 4: [K1, m1, k1, m1, k1] twice. (10 sts)

Rounds 5–7: Knit.

Stuff cheek.

Round 8: [K2tog, k1, k2tog] twice. (6 sts)

Round 9: Knit.

Round 10: [S1 k2tog psso] twice. (2 sts)

Break yarn, weave loose end through remaining stitches, knot, pull knot to inside of fabric to secure.

SMALL CHEEK TRIM (make 2)

Using US 5 (3.75mm) DPNs and **A**, CO 4 sts, PM, join to knit in the round.

Round 1: Knit.

Round 2: [K1, m1, k1] twice. (6 sts)

Rounds 3–5: Knit.

Stuff.

Round 6: [K2tog, k1] twice. (4 sts)

Round 7: [K2tog] twice. (2 sts)

Break yarn, pull tail through remaining sts, and pull loose end into inside of fabric.

RIGHT EAR

Using US 5 (3.75mm) DPNs and **A**, CO 12 sts, PM, join to knit in the round.

Rounds 1–2: Knit.

Round 3: [K3, m1, k2, m1, k1] twice. (16 sts)

Rounds 4–6: Knit.

Round 7: [K1, m1, k2, m1, k4, m1, k1] twice. (22 sts)

(continued right column)

Rounds 8–10: Knit.

Round 11: [K4, m1, k6, m1, k1] twice. (26 sts)

Rounds 12–16: Knit.

Switch to **C**.

Rounds 17–19: Knit.

Switch to **B**.

Round 20: Knit.

Round 21: [K4, k2tog, k4, k2tog, k1] twice. (22 sts)

Rounds 22–24: Knit.

Round 25: [K1, k2tog, k1, k2tog, k2, k2tog, k1] twice. (16 sts)

Rounds 26–28: Knit.

Stuff ear.

Round 29: [K3, k2tog, k2tog, k1] twice. (12 sts)

Rounds 30–32: Knit.

Round 33: [K2tog] 6 times. (6 sts)

Round 34: Knit.

Round 35: [K2tog] 3 times. (3 sts)

Break yarn, pull tail through remaining sts, and pull loose end into inside of fabric.

LEFT EAR

Using US 5 (3.75mm) DPNs and **A**, CO 12 sts, PM, join to knit in the round.

Round 1: Knit.

Round 2: [K3, m1, k2, m1, k1] twice. (16 sts)

Rounds 3–4: Knit.

Round 5: [K3, m1, k4, m1, k1] twice. (20 sts)

Rounds 6–7: Knit.

Round 8: [K1, m1, k2, m1, k6, m1, k1] twice. (26 sts)

Rounds 9–10: Knit.

Round 11: [K4, m1, k8, m1, k1] twice. (30 sts)

Round 12: Knit.

FEET

LEGS

LARGE CHEEK TRIM

SMALL CHEEK TRIM

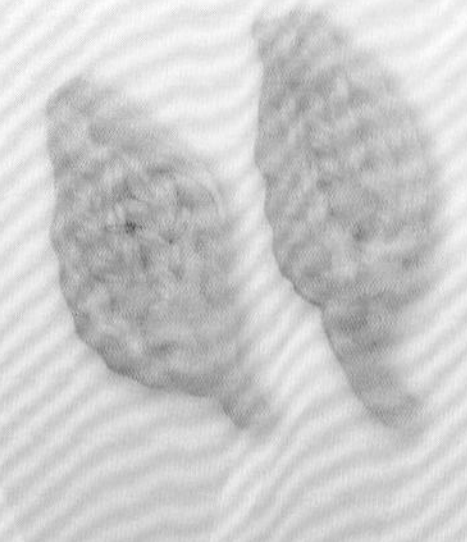

Divide for ear trim:

Round 13: K23, place next 7 sts on scrap yarn, removing marker as you go. (23 sts)

Round 14: PM, CO 3 sts, knit to end. (26 sts)

Rounds 15–16: Knit.

Switch to **C**.

Rounds 17–19: Knit.

Switch to **B**.

Round 20: Knit.

Round 21: [K4, k2tog, k4, k2tog, k1] twice. (22 sts)

Rounds 22–24: Knit.

Round 25: [K1, k2tog, k1, k2tog, k2, k2tog, k1] twice. (16 sts)

Rounds 26–28: Knit.

Stuff ear.

Round 29: [K3, k2tog, k2tog, k1] twice. (12 sts)

Rounds 30–32: Knit.

Round 33: [K2tog] 6 times. (6 sts)

Round 34: Knit.

Round 35: [K2tog] 3 times. (3 sts)

Break yarn, pull tail through remaining sts, and pull loose end into inside of fabric.

Place 7 sts from scrap yarn back on DPNs.

Round 1: K7, pick up and knit 3 sts from inside edge of ear. (10 sts)

Round 2: Knit.

Round 3: [K2, k2tog, k1] twice. (8 sts)

Rounds 4–6: Knit.

Stuff ear.

Round 7: [K2tog] 4 times. (4 sts)

Break yarn, pull tail through remaining sts, and pull loose end into inside of fabric.

NECK TRIM

Using US 5 (3.75mm) DPNs and **B**, CO 3 sts.

Knit a 3½in (9cm) i-cord. BO.

TAIL

Using US 5 (3.75mm) DPNs and **A**, CO 4 sts, PM, join to knit in the round.

Round 1: [Kfb] 4 times. (8 sts)

Rounds 2–4: Knit.

Round 5: [K2tog] 4 times. (4 sts)

Break yarn, pull tail through remaining sts, and pull loose end into inside of fabric.

ASSEMBLY

Cut out all felt pieces using templates.

Use images as guides for positioning.

Glue felt pieces for eyes, nose, sole of feet, and ears.

Use **D** to sew a 1in (2.5cm) line across center of face in the shape of a small smile.

Sew a ½in (1.25cm) vertical line above smile.

Use orange embroidery thread to embroider nose.

Sew ears to top of head.

Sew cheek trims to sides of head, with one large and one small on each side as shown.

Sew tail to body.

Sew legs to bottom of body.

Sew feet to legs.

Sew arms to body.

Sew neck trim to neck.

Use **D** to outline toes and fingers.

Be sure to weave in all ends to ensure a smooth finish.

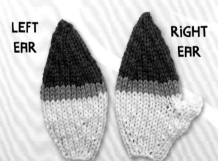

LEFT EAR

RIGHT EAR

NECK TRIM

TAIL

PiPLUP

OFFICIAL COLORS

NATIONAL POKÉDEX NO.	TYPE	WEIGHT	HEIGHT
0393	Water	11.5 lbs/ 5.2 kg	1 ft 4 in/ 0.4 m

Piplup doesn't like to be taken care of. It's difficult to bond with since it won't listen to its Trainer.

MATERIALS

- Cascade 220 (100% wool), 10 to ply/aran, 100g (220yd/200m), in the following shade:
- Robin Egg Blue (8905); 100yd/92m (**A**)
- White (8505); 100yd/92m (**B**)
- Blue Velvet (7818); 100yd/92m (**C**)
- Goldenrod (7827); 50yd/45m (**D**)
- Set of 5 US size 5 (3.75mm) DPNs
- Felt pieces in black, white, and blue
- Felt glue
- Polyester filling

GAUGE

22 sts and 26 rows measure 4 x 4in (10 x 10cm) over stockinette stitch (stocking stitch) using US 5 (3.75mm) needles.

FINISHED SIZE

7in (18cm) tall

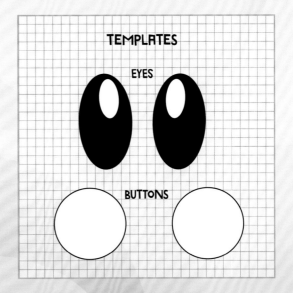

TEMPLATES

EYES

BUTTONS

HEAD

Using US 5 (3.75mm) DPNs and **A**, CO 4 sts, PM, join to knit in the round.

Round 1: [Kfb] 4 times. (8 sts)

Round 2: [Kfb] 8 times. (16 sts)

Round 3: Knit.

Divide sts evenly over 4 DPNs, 4 sts on each needle.

Round 4: [K1, m1, k2, m1, k]) 4 times. (24 sts)

Round 5: Knit.

Round 6: [K2, m1, k2, m1, k2] 4 times. (32 sts)

Round 7: Knit

Round 8: [K3, m1, knit to last 3 sts on current needle, m1, k3] 4 times. (40 sts)

Repeat rounds 7–8 three times more, until you have 64 sts, 16 on each needle.

Rounds 15–17: Knit.

Round 18: [K3, m1, knit to last 3 sts on current needle, m1, k3] 4 times. (72 sts)

Rounds 19–31: Knit.

Round 32: [K3, k2tog, knit to last 5 sts on needle, k2tog, k3] 4 times. (64 sts)

Rounds 33–35: Knit.

Round 36: [K3, k2tog, knit to last 5 sts on needle, k2tog, k3] 4 times. (56 sts)

Round 37: Knit.

Repeat: Repeat rounds 34–35 three more times, until you have 32 sts, 8 on each needle.

Pause to stuff the head until almost full.

Round 44: [K2, k2tog, k2tog, k2] 4 times. (24 sts)

Round 45: Knit.

Round 46: [K1, k2tog, k2tog, k1] 4 times. (16 sts)

Finish stuffing head.

Round 47: [K2tog] 8 times. (8 sts)

Round 48: [K2tog] 4 times. (4 sts)

Break yarn, weave loose end through remaining sts, knot, pull knot to inside of fabric to secure.

BODY

Using US 5 (3.75mm) DPNs and **A**, CO 44 sts, PM, join to knit in the round.

Round 1: [Kfb] 4 times. (8 sts)

Round 2: [Kfb] 8 times. (16 sts)

Round 3: Knit.

Divide sts evenly over 4 dpns, 4 sts on each needle.

Round 4: [K1, m1, k2, m1, k]) 4 times. (24 sts)

Round 5: Knit.

Round 6: [K2, m1, k2, m1, k2] 4 times. (32 sts)

Round 7: Knit

Round 8: [K3, m1, knit to last 3 sts on current needle, m1, k3] 4 times. (40 sts) .

Repeat rounds 7–8 one more time until you have 48 sts, 12 on each needle.

Rounds 11–26: Knit.

Round 27: [K5, k2tog, k5] 4 times. (44 sts)

Rounds 28–30: Knit.

Round 31: As round 27. 40 sts, 10 on each needle.

Round 32: Knit.

BO. Stuff body.

FACE STRIPE

Using US 5 (3.75mm) DPNs and **A**, CO 10 sts.

Row 1: Knit.

Row 2: Purl.

Row 3: [K4, k2tog, k4]. (9 sts)

Continue in stockinette st, decreasing 1 st in the middle of the row on every 3rd row until you have 5 sts. BO. Press lightly.

HOOD

Using US 5 (3.75mm) DPNs and **C**, CO 4 sts, PM, join to knit in the round.

Round 1: [Kfb] 4 times. (8 sts)

Round 2: [Kfb] 8 times. (16 sts)

Round 3: Knit.

Divide sts evenly over 4 DPNs, 4 sts on each needle.

Round 4: [K1, m1, k2, m1, k]) 4 times. (24 sts)

Round 5: Knit.

Round 6: [K2, m1, k2, m1, k2] 4 times. (32 sts)

Round 7: Knit

Round 8: [K3, m1, knit to last 3 sts on current needle, m1, k3] 4 times. (40 sts) .

Round 9: Knit.

Round 10: [K3, m1, knit to last 3 sts on current needle, m1, k3] 4 times. (48 sts)

Round 11: Knit.

Split hood for front and back:

Round 12: [K10, BO 3 sts (1 st on RN), K9, place these last 10 sts on scrap yarn, BO 3 sts, (1st st left on RN, move this st to LN)

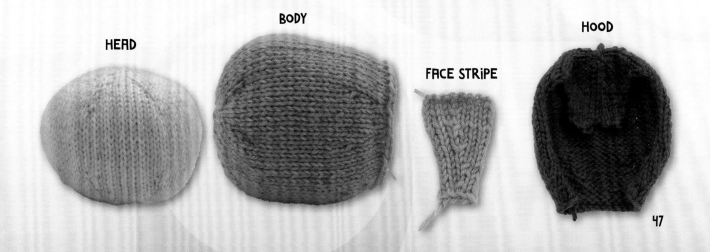

HEAD   BODY   FACE STRIPE   HOOD

k2tog, k5, m1, k6, m1, k6, m1, k3, remove end of round marker, continue knitting back of cape flat over the first 10 sts worked in this round as follows: k3, m1, k5, k2tog], turn to continue working in rows. (34 sts)

Row 13 (WS): [P2tog, purl to last 2 sts, p2tog]. (32 sts)

Row 14: [K2tog, k4, m1, k6, m1, k8, m1, k6, m1, k4, k2tog]. (34 sts)

Row 15: Purl.

Row 16: [K2tog, knit to last 2 sts, k2tog]. (32 sts)

Row 17: Purl.

Row 18: [K2tog, k3, m1, k6, m1, k10, m1, k6, m1, k3, k2tog]. (34 sts)

Rows 19-29: Work in stockinette st, starting with a purl row.

Row 30: [K1, m1, k2, k2tog, k6, k2tog, k8, k2tog, k6, k2tog, k2, m1, k1]. (32 sts)

Rows 31–33: Work in stockinette st, starting with a purl row

Row 34: [K1, m1, k2, k2tog, k6, k2tog, k6, k2tog, k6, k2tog, k2, m1, k1]. (30 sts)

Row 35: Purl

Round 36: [K1, m1, k2, k2tog, k6, k2tog, k4, k2tog, k6, k2tog, k2, m1, k1]. (28 sts)

Row 37: Purl.

Row 38: [K1, m1, k2, k2tog, k6, k2tog, k2, k2tog, k6, k2tog, k2, m1, k1]. (26 sts)

Round 39: Purl.

BO.

Place 10 sts from scrap yarn on a DPN with RS facing.

Beginning with a knit row, work 4 rows in stockinette st.

CAPE SPIKES

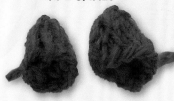

Divide for trim:

Row 5: [K2tog, k1, k2tog, turn leaving remaining sts unworked. (8 sts)

Row 6: [P3tog]. (5 sts)

Pull tail through last st and weave in loose end.

Woth RS facing, join working yarn to remaining 5 sts.

Repeat: Repeat rows 5 and 6.

Pull tail through last st and weave in loose end.

CAPE FRONT

Using US 5 (3.75mm) DPNs and **C**, CO 4 sts, PM, join to knit in the round.

Round 1: [Kfb] 4 times. (8 sts)

Round 2: [Kfb, k1] 4 times. (12 sts)

Round 3: [Kfb, k3, kfb, k1] twice. (16 sts)

Round 4: Knit.

Round 5: [Kfb, k5, kfb, k1] twice. (20 sts)

Round 6: Knit.

Place these 20 sts on scrap yarn and set aside.

Using US 5 (3.75mm) DPNs and **C**, CO 4 sts, PM, join to knit in the round.

Repeat rounds 1–6.

Connect front edges of cape:

Round 7: [K10, k20 from scrap yarn, k10]. (40 sts)

Round 8: [Kfb, k17, kfb, k1] twice. (44 sts)

Round 9: Knit.

Round 10: [Kfb, k19, kfb, k1] twice. (48 sts)

Round 11: Knit.

Round 12: [Kfb, k21, kfb, k1] twice. (52 sts)

BO, leaving a long tail for seaming. Stuff pockets of front edge of cape lightly, and sew closed with a long seam across the top.

CAPE BACK

Using US 5 (3.75mm) DPNs and **C**, CO 56sts, PM, join to knit in the round.

Rounds 1–4: Knit.

Round 5: [K1, k2tog, k22, k2tog, k1] twice. (52 sts)

Rounds 6– 7: Knit.

Round 8: [K1, k2tog, k20, k2tog, k1] twice. (48 sts)

Rounds 9–10: Knit.

Round 11: [K1, k2tog, k18, k2tog, k1] twice. (44 sts)

Rounds 12–13: Knit.

Round 14: [K1, k2tog, k16, k2tog, k1] twice. (40 sts)

Round 15: Knit.

Round 16: [K1, k2tog, k14, k2tog, k1] twice. (36 sts)

Round 17: Knit.

Round 18: [K1, k2tog, k12, k2tog, k1] twice. (32 sts)

Round 19: [K1, k2tog, k10, k2tog, k1] twice. (28 sts)

Round 20: [K1, k2tog, k8, k2tog, k1] twice. (24 sts)

Round 21: [K2tog, k2tog, k4, k2tog, k2tog] twice. (16 sts)

Divide sts evenly between 2 dpns. Use kitchener st to graft together.

Stuff lightly. Seam cast-on edge closed.
.

CAPE SPIKES (make 2)

Using US 5 (3.75mm) DPNs and **C**, CO 10sts, PM, join to knit in the round.

Round 1: Knit.

Round 2: [K2tog, k3] twice. 8 sts

Round 3: Knit.

Round 4: [K2tog, k2] twice. 6 sts

CAPE FRONT

CAPE BACK

Round 5: Knit.

Round 6: [K2tog, k1] twice. 4 sts

Round 7: [K2tog] twice. 2 sts

Break yarn, weave loose end through remaining stitches, knot, pull knot to inside of fabric to secure. Stuff spikes.

WINGS (make 2)

Using US 5 (3.75mm) DPNs and **A**, CO 10sts, PM, join to knit in the round.

Rounds 1–2: Knit.

Round 3: [K1, m1, k3, m1, k1] twice. (14 sts)

Rounds 4–6: Knit.

Round 7: [K1, m1, k5, m1, k1] twice. (18 sts)

Rounds 8–10: Knit.

Round 11: [K1, k2tog, k3, k2tog, k1] twice. (14 sts)

Rounds 12–14: Knit.

Round 15: [K1, k2tog, k1, k2tog, k1] twice. (10 sts)

Rounds 16–18: Knit.

Round 19: [K2tog, k1, k2tog] twice. (6 sts)

Round 20: [K2tog] 3 times. (3 sts)

Break yarn, weave loose end through remaining sts, knot, pull knot to inside of fabric to secure.

BEAK

Using US 5 (3.75mm) DPNs and **D**, CO 24 sts, PM, join to knit in the round.

Round 1: Knit.

Round 2: [K2, k2tog, k2] 4 times. (20 sts)

Round 3: [K1, k2tog, k2] 4 times. (16 sts)

Round 4: [K1, k2tog, k1] 4 times. (12 sts)

Round 5: [K1, k2tog] 4 times. (8 sts)

Round 6: K2tog 4 times. 4 sts

Break yarn, weave loose end through remaining sts, knot, pull knot to inside of fabric to secure.

ANKLES (make 2)

Using US 5 (3.75mm) DPNs and **A**, CO 16 sts, PM, join to knit in the round.

Round 1: Knit.

Round 2: [K1, k2tog, k1] 4 times. 12 sts

Round 3: Knit.

BO.

FEET (make 2)

Using US 5 (3.75mm) DPNs and **D**, CO 6 sts, PM, join to knit in the round.

Round 1: Knit.

Round 2: [K1, m1, k2] twice. (8 sts)

Round 3–14: Knit.

Round 15: [K1, k2tog, k1] twice. (6 sts)

Round 16: [K2tog] 3 times. (3 sts)

Break yarn, weave loose end through remaining sts, knot, pull knot to inside of fabric to secure.

ASSEMBLY

Cut out all felt pieces using templates.

Using images as guides for positioning.

Sew head to body.

Sew face stripe down the center of the head.

Sew hood to head, lining up the indentation with the face stripe.

Sew wings on each side of body.

Connect front of cape and back of cape at sides and seam into place.

Sew spikes onto back of cape.

Sew beak onto face, stuffing as you go.

Seam ankles to body.

Seam feet to ankles.

Secure felt eyes to face and buttons to body using felt glue.

WINGS

BEAK

ANKLES

FEET

CHARMANDER

OFFICIAL COLORS

NATIONAL POKÉDEX NO.	TYPE	WEIGHT	HEIGHT
0004	Fire	18.7 lbs/ 8.5 g	2 ft 0 in/ 0.6 m

If Charmander is healthy, the flame on the tip of its tail will burn vigorously and won't go out even if it gets a bit wet.

MATERIALS

- Cascade 220 (100% wool), 10-ply/ aran, 100g (220yd/200m), in the following shades:
- Blaze (9542); 1 ball (**A**)
- Lemon Yellow (4147); 100yd/91m (**B**)
- White (8505); 10yd/9m (**C**)
- Bright Red (8414); 10yd/9m (**D**)
- Black embroidery thread
- Set of five size US 5 (3.75mm) DPNs
- Felt pieces in black, white, yellow, and blue
- Small crochet hook
- Felt brush or toothbrush
- Fabric glue
- Polyester filling

GAUGE

22 sts and 26 rows measure 4 x 4in (10 x 10cm) over stockinette stitch (stocking stitch) using size US 5 (3.75mm) needles

FINISHED SIZE

8½in (21cm) tall

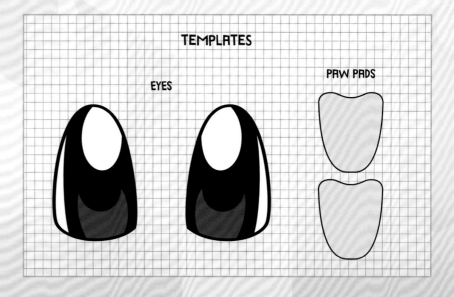

TEMPLATES

EYES

PAW PADS

BODY (worked from bottom up)

Using US 5 (3.75mm) DPNs and **A**, CO 8 sts, PM, join to knit in the round.

Round 1: [Kfb] 8 times. 16 sts

Divide sts evenly between 4 DPNs, 4 sts per needle.

Round 2 and all even-numbered rounds: Knit.

Round 3: [K1, m1, k2, m1, k1] 4 times. (24 sts)

Round 5: [K2, m1, k2, m1, k2] 4 times. (32 sts)

Round 7: [K3, m1, knit to last 3 sts on DPN, m1, k3] 4 times. (40 sts)

Repeat rounds 7 and 8 twice more until you have 56 sts, 14 per needle.

Rounds 13–15: Knit.

Round 16: [K3, m1, knit to last 3 sts on DPN, m1, k3] 4 times. (64 sts)

Rounds 17–28: Knit.

Round 29: [K3, k2tog, knit to last 5 sts on needle, k2tog, k3] 4 times. (56 sts)

Rounds 30–34: Knit.

Repeat rounds 29–34 until you have 32 sts, 8 on each needle. BO.

HEAD

Using US 5 (3.75mm) DPNs and **A**, CO 8 sts, PM, join to knit in the round.

Round 1: [Kfb] 8 times. (16 sts)

Divide sts evenly between 4 DPNs, 4 sts per needle.

BODY

Round 2 and all even numbered rounds: Knit.

Round 3: [K1, m1, k2, m1, k1] 4 times. (24 sts)

Round 5: [K2, m1, k2, m1, k2] 4 times. (32 sts)

Round 7: [K3, m1, knit to last 3 sts on needle, m1, k3] 4 times. (40 sts)

Rounds 13–27: Knit.

Repeat rounds 7–8 twice more until you have 56 sts, 14 per needle.

Round 28: K24, m1, k6, m1, k24. (58 sts)

Round 29: Knit.

Round 30: K11, m1, k6, m1, k24, m1, k6, m1, k11. (62 sts)

Round 31: Knit.

Round 32: K12, m1, k6, m1, k10, m1, k6, m1, k10, m1, k6, m1, k12. (68 sts)

Round 33: Knit.

Round 34: K13, m1, k6, m1, k30, m1, k6, m1, k13. (72 sts)

Round 35: Knit.

Round 36: K14, m1, k6, m1, k13, m1, k6, m1, k13, m1, k6, m1, k14. (78 sts)

Rounds 37–39: Knit.

Round 40: K34, k2tog, k6, k2tog, k34. (76 sts)

Round 41: Knit.

Round 42: K13, k2tog, k6, k2tog, k10, k2tog, k6, k2tog, k10, k2tog, k6, k2tog, k13. (70 sts)

Round 43: Knit.

Round 44: K12, k2tog, k6, k2tog, k8, k2tog, k6, k2tog, k8, k2tog, k6, k2tog, k12. (64 sts)

Round 45: Knit.

Round 46: [K3, k2tog, k6, k2tog, k3] 4 times. (56 sts)

Round 47: Knit.

Round 48: [K3, k2tog, k4, k2tog, k3] 4 times. (48 sts)

Round 49: Knit.

Round 50: [K3, k2tog, k2, k2tog, k3] 4 times. (40 sts)

Round 51: [K2, k2tog, k2, k2tog, k2] 4 times. (32 sts)

BO. Leave long tail for seaming. Stuff head.

FEET (make 2)

Using US 5 (3.75mm) DPNs and **A**, CO 8 sts, PM, join to knit in the round. Divide sts evenly between 4 DPNs, 2 sts per needle.

Round 1: [Kfb, k1] 4 times. (12 sts)

Round 2: Knit.

Round 3: [K1, m1, k4, m1, k1] twice. (16 sts)

Rounds 4–9: Knit.

Round 10: [K1, m1, knit to last st, m1, k1]. (18 sts)

Rounds 11–12: Knit.

Switch to **C**.

Round 13: Knit.

Divide for toes:

First toe

Put the first 3 sts on one DPN, place the next 12 sts on a piece of scrap yarn, put the last 3 sts on another DPN. (6 sts)

*Next round: Knit.

Next round: [S1, k2tog, psso] twice. (2 sts)

Break yarn, pull tail through these two sts, pull loose end into inside of foot.

HEAD

FEET

Second toe

Place first 3 sts from scrap yarn onto a DPN, place the last three sts from scrap yarn onto a 2nd DPN. Reattach white yarn. Repeat between (*****) as for first toe.

Third toe

Place remaining sts on 2 DPNs. Reattach white yarn and complete between (*****) as for first two toes.

Weave in loose ends.

LEGS (make 2)

Left leg

Using US 5 (3.75mm) DPNs and **A**, CO 24 sts, PM, join to knit in the round.

Round 1: K7, k2tog, k1, kfb, k7, kfb, k2, k2tog, k1.

Round 2: Knit.

Repeat rounds 1 and 2 twice more.

Round 7: K7, k2tog, k1, kfb, k7, BO 6 sts. Remove marker. (18 sts)
Continue knitting in rows.

Row 8: K16, k2tog. (17 sts)

Row 9: P15, p2tog. (16 sts)

Row 10: K5, kfb, k2, k2tog, k4, k2tog. (15 sts)

Row 11: P13, p2tog. (14 sts)

Row 12: K4, kfb, k2, k2tog, k3, k2tog. (13 sts)

Row 13: P11, p2tog. (12 sts)

Row 14: K3, kfb, k2, k2tog, k2, k2tog. (11 sts)

Row 15: P9, p2tog. (10 sts)

Row 16: K2, kfb, k2, k2tog, k1, k2tog. (9 sts)

Row 17: P7, p2tog. (8 sts)

Row 18: K2tog, k4, k2tog. (6 sts)

BO. Leave long tail for seaming.

Right leg

Using US 5 (3.75mm) DPNs and **A**, CO 24 sts, PM, join to knit in the round.

Round 1: K7, k2tog, k1, kfb, k7, kfb, k2, k2tog, k1.

Round 2: Knit.

Repeat rounds 1 and 2 twice more.

Round 7: K6, BO 6 sts, (1 st left on right needle after cast off), k5, kfb, k2, k2tog, k1. Remove marker. (18 sts)

Row 8: K4, k2tog, turn. (17 sts)
Continue knitting in rows.

Row 9: P15, p2tog. (16 sts)

Row 10: K6, k2tog, k1,kfb, k4, k2tog. (15 sts)

Row 11: P13, p2tog. (14 sts)

Row 12: K5, k2tog, k1,kfb ,k3, k2tog. (13 sts)

Row 13: P11, p2tog. (12 sts)

Row 14: K4, k2tog, k1,kfb ,k2, k2tog. (11 sts)

Row 15: P9, p2tog. (10 sts)

Row 16: K2, kfb, k2, k2tog, k1, k2tog. (9 sts)

Row 17: P7, p2tog. (8 sts)

Row 18: K2tog, k4, k2tog. (6 sts)

BO. Leave long tail for seaming.

ARMS (make 2)

Using US 5 (3.75mm) DPNs and **A**, CO 7 sts.

Row 1 (WS): Purl.

Row 2: K1, m1, knit to last st, m1, k1. (9 sts)

Repeat rows 1–2. (11 sts)

Row 5: Purl.

Row 6: K11, CO11, pm, join to knit in the round. (22 sts)

Rounds 7-10: Knit.

Round 11: [K4, k2tog, k5] twice. (20 sts)

Rounds 12–20: Knit.

Round 21: [K1, k2tog, k4, k2tog, k1] twice. (16 sts)

Rounds 22–23: Knit.

Split for fingers

Divide sts evenly between 2 DPNs, 8 on each needle.

Next round: K2tog, leave next 12 sts on DPNs or scrap yarn, K2tog. (2 sts)

Break yarn, pull tail through st to make 1st finger.

Reattach working yarn.

Next round: K2tog, leave next 8 sts on DPNs or scrap yarn, K2tog. (2 sts)

Break yarn, pull tail through st to make 2nd finger.

Reattach working yarn.

Next round: K2tog, leave next 8 sts on DPNs or scrap yarn, K2tog. (2 sts)

Break yarn, pull tail through st to make 3rd finger.

Reattach working yarn.

Next round: [K2tog] twice. (2 sts)

Break yarn, pull tail through remaining sts to make last finger.

Weave in loose ends. Stuff arm.

TAIL

Using US 5 (3.75mm) DPNs and **A**, CO 30 sts, PM, join to knit in the round.

Rounds 1–2: Knit.

Round 3: [K2tog, k8] 3 times. (27 sts)

Rounds 4–5: Knit.

Round 6: [K2tog, k7] 3 times. (24 sts)

Row 7: K6, wrap and turn

Row 8: P6, SM, p6, wrap and turn.

Row 9: K6, SM, k4, wrap and turn.

Row 10: P4, SM, p4, wrap and turn.

LEGS   ARMS   TAIL

Row 11: K4, SM, k2, wrap and turn.

Row 12: P2, SM, p2, wrap and turn.

Row 13: K2, SM, knit all around to marker, picking up wraps as you go.

Row 14: [K1, k2tog, knit to last 3 sts, k2tog, k1. (22 sts)

Rounds 15–18: Knit.

Round 19: K1, k2tog, knit to last 3 sts, k2tog, k1. (20 sts)

Round 20: K5, wrap and turn.

Round 21: P5, SM, p5, wrap and turn.

Round 22: K5, SM, k3, wrap and turn.

Round 23: P3, SM, p3, wrap and turn.

Round 24: K3, SM, k1, wrap and turn.

Round 25: P1, SM, p1, wrap and turn.

Round 26: K1, SM, knit to marker, picking up wraps as you go.

Round 27: K1, k2tog, knit till 3 sts remain, k2tog, k1. (18 sts)

Rounds 28–31: Knit.

Round 32: K1, k2tog, knit till 3 sts remain k2tog, k1.* (16 sts)

Round 33: K3, wrap and turn.

Round 34: P3, SM, p3, wrap and turn.

Round 35: K3, SM, k2, wrap and turn.

Round 36: P2, SM, p2, wrap and turn.

Round 37: K2, SM, k1, wrap and turn.

Round 38: P1, SM, p1, wrap and turn.

Round 39: K1, SM, knit all around to marker, picking up wraps as you go.

Repeat rounds 27–39 twice. (8 sts)

Next round: [K2tog, k2] twice. (6 sts)

Next round: [K2tog] 3 times. (3 sts)

Break yarn, pull tail through remaining sts and pull loose end into inside of fabric. Block then stuff tail to smooth out lumps from short rows.

STRiPE

Using US 5 (3.75mm) DPNs and **B**, CO 8 sts.

Row 1: [Kfb, k5, kfb, k1]. (10 sts)

Row 2: Purl.

Row 3: [K1, m1, knit to last stitch, m1, k1]. (12 sts)

Row 4: Purl.

Repeat rows 3–4 twice more until you have 16 sts.

Work in stockinette st for 18 rows.

Row 27: [K1, k2tog, knit to last 2 sts, k2tog, k1]. (14 sts)

Rows 28 to 32: Work in stockinette st.

Repeat rows 27–32. (12 sts)

Row 39: [K1, k2tog, knit to last 2 sts, k2tog, k1]. (10 sts)

Work 26 rows in stockinette st.

Row 66: [K1, k2tog, knit to last 2 sts, k2tog, k1]. (8 sts)

Work 18 rows in stockinette st.

Row 85: [K1, k2tog, knit to last 2 sts, k2tog, k1]. (6 sts)

Row 86: Purl.

Row 87: [K1, k2tog twice, k1]. (4 sts)

Row 88: [P2tog] twice. (2 sts)

Break yarn leaving long tail for seaming. Pull tail through last 2 sts.

ASSEMBLY

Cut out all felt pieces using templates.

Use images as guides for positioning.

Glue felt pieces for eyes.

Glue felt pieces for soles.

Sew head to body.

Sew tail to body.

Sew stripe to body and tail.

Sew legs to body.

Sew feet to legs.

Sew arms to body.

Cut several 4in (10cm) strands of yarn in **D** and **B**.

Fold a strand in half and use crochet hook to pull through tip of tail, (see figure 1 below). Brush out strands to create flame.

Use black embroidery thread to embroider mouth and nostrils.

Be sure to weave in all ends to ensure a smooth finish.

figure 1

STRiPE

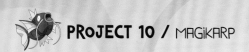

MAGIKARP

OFFICIAL COLORS

NATIONAL POKÉDEX NO.	TYPE	WEIGHT	HEIGHT
0129	Water	22.0 lbs/ 10.0 kg	2 ft 11 in/ 0.9 m

An underpowered, pathetic Pokémon. It may jump high on rare occasions but never more than seven feet.

MATERIALS

- Cascade 220 (100% wool), 10-ply/ aran, 100g (220yd/200m), in the following shades:
- Tiger Lily (9605); 1 ball (**A**)
- Butter (8687); 110yd/100m (**B**)
- White (8505); 110yd/100m (**C**)
- Shrimp (7804); Oddments (**D**)
- Black (8555); Oddments (**E**)
- Set of five size US 5 (3.75mm) DPNs
- Felt pieces in black and white
- Fabric glue
- Polyester filling

GAUGE

22 sts and 26 rows measure 4 x 4in (10 x 10cm) over stockinette stitch (stocking stitch) using size US 5 (3.75mm) needles.

FINISHED SIZE

8.5in (21.6 cm) long

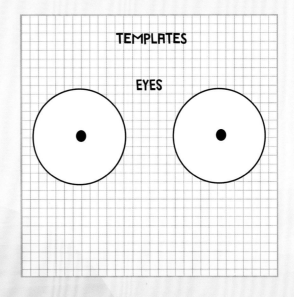

TEMPLATES

EYES

BODY (worked from front to back)

Using US 5 (3.75mm) DPNs and **A**, CO 4 sts, PM, join to knit in the round.

Round 1: [Kfb] 4 times. (8 sts)

Round 2: [Kfb] 8 times. (16 sts)

Round 3: Knit.

Round 4: [K1, m1, k2, m1, k1] 4 times. (24 sts)

Round 5: Knit.

Round 6: [K2, m1, k2, m1, k2] 4 times. (32 sts)

Round 7: Knit.

Round 8: [K2, m1, k4, m1, k2] 4 times. (40 sts)

Round 9: Knit.

Round 10: [K2, m1, k6, m1, k2] 4 times. (48 sts)

Round 11: Knit.

Round 12: [K2, m1, k8, m1, k2] 4 times. (56 sts)

Round 13: Knit.

Round 14: [K2, m1, k10, m1, k2] 4 times. (64 sts)

Round 15: Knit.

Round 16: [K2, m1, k12, m1, k18] twice. (68 sts)

Round 17: Knit.

Round 18: [K2, m1, k14, m1, k18] twice. (72 sts)

Rounds 19–31: Knit.

Round 32: [K2, k2tog, k12, k2tog, k18] twice. (68 sts)

Rounds 33–35: Knit.

Round 36: [K2, k2tog, k10, k2tog, k4, k2tog, k8, k2tog, k2] twice. (60 sts)

Round 37–39: Knit.

Round 40: [K2, k2tog, k8, k2tog, k16] twice. (56 sts)

Round 41: Knit.

Round 42: [K2, k2tog, k6, k2tog, k2] 4 times. (48 sts)

Round 43: Knit.

Round 44: [K2, k2tog, k4, k2tog, k14] twice. (44 sts)

Round 45: Knit.

Round 46: [K2, k2tog, k2, k2tog, k4, k2tog, k4, k2tog, k2] twice. (36 sts) Stuff body.

Rounds 47–49: Knit.

Round 50: [K2tog, k4, k2tog, k10] twice. (32 sts)

Round 51: Knit.

Round 52: K7, k2tog, k4, k2tog, k8, k2tog, k4, k2tog, k1. (28 sts)

Round 53: Knit.

Round 54: K7, k2tog, k2, k2tog, k8, k2tog, k2, k2tog, k1. (24 sts)

Round 55: Knit.

Round 56: [K6, k2tog, k2, k2tog] twice. (20 sts)

BO. Stuff completely.

BODY MIDDLE BAND

Using US 5 (3.75mm) DPNs and **A**, pick up and knit 72 sts around the middle of the body in a straight line. PM, join to knit in the round.

Knit 5 rows. BO, leaving long tail. Use tail to sew bound-off edge to body.

TAIL FIN

Using US 5 (3.75mm) DPNs and **C**, CO 20 sts, PM, join to knit in the round. Divide sts evenly between two DPNs, (10 sts on each)

Round 1: [Kfb, knit to last 2 sts on DPN, kfb, k1] twice. (24 sts)

Repeat round 1 until you have 40 sts, 20 on each needle.

Rounds 6–7: Knit.

Round 8: [Kfb, knit to last 2 sts on DPN, kfb, k1] twice. (44 sts)

Round 9-11: Knit.

Divide for back of tail:

Round 12: Kfb, k10, place next 22 sts on scrap yarn, k9, kfb, k1. (24 sts)

*Round 13: K10, k2tog twice, k10. (22 sts)

BODY

BODY MIDDLE BAND

TAIL FIN

Round 14: Kfb, k19, kfb, k1. 24 sts

Round 15: K10, k2tog twice, k10. (22 sts)

Round 16: Kfb, k8, k2tog twice, k7, kfb, k1. Close up opening with kitchener stitch.**

Divide remaining 22 sts between 2 DPNs. Reattach working yarn to outer edge of fin.

Round 12: Kfb, k19, kfb, k1. (24 sts)

Rounds 13–16: Repeat from * to **. Press fin. Sew back edge closed.

TAIL FIN TRIM (make 2)

Using US 5 (3.75mm) DPNs and **A**, CO 6 sts

Row 1: Knit.

Rows 2–8: Work even in stockinette st.

Row 9: K2, k2tog, k2. (5 sts)

Rows 10–14: Work even in stockinette st

Row 15: K1, k2tog, k2. (4 sts)

Row 18–20: Work even in stockinette st

Row 21: K1, k2tog, k1. (3 sts)

Row 22: Purl.

Row 23: Knit.

Row 24: Purl.

Row 25: Sl, k2tog, psso. (1 st)

Break yarn, pull tail through remaining st. Press lightly.

TOP FIN

Using US 5 (3.75mm) DPNs and **B**, CO 32 sts, PM, join to knit in the round. Divide sts evenly between two DPNs, (16 sts on each)

Round 1: Knit.

Round 2: [K1, m1, k14, m1, k1] twice. (36 sts)

Round 3: Knit.

Round 4: [K1, m1, k16, m1, k1] twice. (40 sts)

Round 5: Knit.

Divide for spikes:

Front spike

Knit first 6 sts from first needle, place next 28 sts on scrap yarn, knit last 6 sts from 2nd needle. Join to knit in the round. (12 st)s

Round 1: K1, m1, k3, k2tog twice, k3, m1, k1.

Round 2: Knit.

Round 3: K4, k2tog twice, k4. (10 sts)

Round 4: Knit.

Round 5: K3, k2tog twice, k3. (8 sts)

Round 6: Knit.

Round 7: K2, k2tog twice, k2. (6 sts)

Round 8: Knit.

Round 9: [K2tog] 3 times. (3 sts)

Break yarn, pull tail through remaining sts and secure.

Middle spike

From scrap yarn, place the next 8 sts on a DPN, then place the last 8 sts on a 2nd DPN. Join to knit in the round. (16 sts)

Round 1: Knit.

Round 2: [K1, k2tog, k2, k2tog, k1] twice. (12 sts)

Rounds 3–4: Knit.

Round 5: [K2, k2tog, k2] twice. (10 sts)

Rounds 6–8: Knit.

Round 9: [K1, k2tog, k2] twice. (8 sts)

Round 10: Knit.

Round 11: [K2tog] 4 times. (4 sts)

Round 12: [K2tog] twice. (2 sts)

Break yarn, pull tail through remaining sts and secure.

Rear spike

Place the remaining 12 sts on 2 DPNs. Reconnect yarn to outside edge.

Round 1: K1, m1, k3, k2tog twice, k3, m1, k1.

Round 2: Knit.

Round 3: K4, k2tog twice, k4. (10 sts)

Round 4: Knit.

Round 5: K3, k2tog twice, k3. (8 sts)

Round 6: Knit.

Round 7: K2, k2tog twice, k2. (6 sts)

Round 8: Knit.

Round 9: [K2tog] 3 times. (3 sts)

Break yarn, pull tail through remaining sts and secure.

TAIL FIN TRIM

TOP FIN

BOTTOM FIN

BOTTOM FIN

Using US 5 (3.75mm) DPNs and **B**, CO 24 sts, PM, join to knit in the round. Divide sts evenly between two DPNs, (12 sts on each)

Round 1: Knit.

Round 2: [K1, m1, k10, m1, k1] twice. (28 sts)

Round 3: Knit.

Round 4: [K1, m1, k12, m1, k1] twice. (32 sts)

Round 5: Knit.

Divide for fin points:

Round 6: K1, m1, k3, place next 24 sts on scrap yarn, k3, m1, k1. (10 sts)

Round 7: K3, k2tog twice, k3. (8 sts)

Round 8: K1, m1, k1, k2tog twice, k1, m1, k1.

Round 9: K2, k2tog twice, k2. (6 sts)

Round 10: [K2tog] 3 times. (3 sts)

Break yarn, pull tail through remaining sts and secure.

Second point:

Place first 4 sts from scrap yarn on a DPN. Place last 4 sts from scrap yarn on a 2nd DPN. (8 sts)

Reattach working yarn next to first fin point. PM, join to knit in the round.

Rounds 6–7: Knit. (8 sts)

Round 8: [K1, k2tog, k1] twice. (6 sts)

Round 9: Knit.

Round 10: [K2tog] 3 times. (3 sts)

Break yarn, pull tail through remaining sts and secure.

Third point:

Place first 4 sts from scrap yarn on a DPN. Place last 4 sts from scrap yarn on a 2nd DPN. (8 sts)

Reattach working yarn next to 2nd fin point. PM, join to knit in the round.

Rounds 6–7: Knit. (8 sts)

Round 8: K2tog, k4, k2tog. (6 sts)

Round 9: Knit.

Round 10: [K2tog] 3 times. (3 sts)

Break yarn, pull tail through remaining sts and secure.

Fourth point:

Split remaining 8 sts on scrap yard evenly between 2 DPNs.

Reattach working yarn next to 3rd fin point. PM, join to knit in the round.

Rounds 6–7: Knit. (8 sts)

Round 8: [K1, k2tog, k1] twice. (6 sts)

Round 9: Knit.

Round 10: [K2tog] 3 times. (3 sts)

Break yarn, pull tail through remaining sts and secure.

SIDE FINS (make 2)

Using US 5 (3.75mm) DPNs and **C**, CO 12 sts, PM, join to knit in the round.

Round 1: Knit.

Round 2: [K1, m1, k4, m1, k1] twice. (16 sts)

Round 3: Knit.

Round 4: [K1, m1, k6, m1, k1] twice. (20 sts)

Rounds 5–6: Knit.

Round 7: [K1, m1, k8, m1, k1] twice. (24 sts)

Rounds 8–10: Knit.

Round 11: [K1, m1, k10, m1, k1] twice. (28 sts)

Round 12: Knit.

Begin short row shaping of fin:

Round 13: K4, wrap and turn.

Round 14: P4, sm, p4, wrap and turn.

Round 15: K4, sm, k2, wrap and turn.

Round 16: P2, sm, p2, wrap and turn.

Round 17: K2, sm, wrap and turn.

Round 18: P18, picking up wraps and knitting them in as you go, wrap and turn.

Round 19: K8, wrap and turn.

Round 20: P6, wrap and turn.

Round 21: K4, wrap and turn.

Round 22: P2, wrap and turn.

Round 23: Knit to marker, picking up wraps and knitting them in as you go.

Round 24: Purl, picking up remaining wraps and knitting them in as you go.

Split sts evenly between 2 DPNs. Close opening with kitchener st.

SIDE FINS

Fin trim

Using **A**, pick up and knit 17 sts along upper edge of fin, then pick up and knit 6 sts from cast on edge. (23 sts)

Knit 1 row. Bind off. Weave in loose ends. Repeat for 2nd fin.

TENTACLES (make 2)

Using US 5 (3.75mm) DPNs and **B**, CO 3 sts.

Knit a 4.9in (12cm) i-cord. BO. Weave in loose ends.

LiPS

Using US 5 (3.75mm) DPNs and **D**, CO 8sts.

Row 1: Kfb, k5, kfb, k1. (10 sts)

Row 2: Pfb, p7, pfb, p1. (12 sts)

Row 3: Kfb, k9, kfb, k1. (14 sts)

Row 4: Purl.

Row 5: K1, k2tog, k8, k2tog, k1. (12 sts)

Row 6: P1, p2tog, p6, p2tog, p1. (10 sts)

Row 7: K1, k2tog, k4, k2tog, k1. (8 sts)

BO purlwise.

ASSEMBLY

Cut out all felt pieces using templates.

Use images as guides for positioning.

Glue eyes to sides of body.

Sew tail fin trim to top and bottom edge of the tail fin. Pointy edge should hang slightly off the ends.

Sew tail fin trim together along edge.

Sew tail to end of body.

Sew top fin to body just behind middle band, and centered along the top.

Sew bottom fin to body just behind middle band, and centered along the bottom edge.

Sew side fins to body.

Sew lips to face. Use matching length of yarn to pull center in, creating two lips, and secure.

Sew tentacles to sides of head near the lips.

Using **E**, embroider pattern on body of fish.

Using **E**, embroider fin lines on tail and side fins.

Be sure to weave in all ends to ensure a smooth finish.

TENTACLES

LiPS

TURTWIG

OFFICIAL COLORS

NATIONAL POKÉDEX No.	TYPE	WEIGHT	HEIGHT
0387	Grass	22.5 lbs/ 10.2 kg	1 ft 4 in/ 0.4 m

It uses its whole body to photosynthesize when exposed to sunlight. Its shell is made from hardened soil.

MATERIALS

- Cascade 220 (100% wool), 10-ply/ aran, 100g (220yd/200m), in the following shades:

- Tender Greens (1034); 1 ball (**A**)

- Neon Yellow (7828); 110yd/ 100m (**B**)

- Sunflower (2415); 110yd/100m (**C**)

- Black (8555); 55yd/50m (**D**)

- Set of five size US 5 (3.75mm) DPNs

- Felt pieces in yellow, green, black, and white

- Fabric glue

- Polyester filling

GAUGE

22 sts and 26 rows measure 4 x 4in (10 x 10cm) over stockinette stitch (stocking stitch) using size US 5 (3.75mm) needles.

FINISHED SIZE

7in (17.8cm) tall

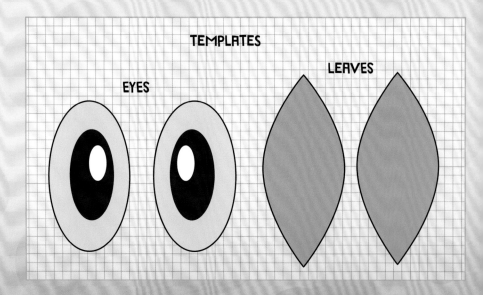

TEMPLATES

EYES

LEAVES

HEAD

US 5 (3.75mm) DPNs and **A**, CO 4 sts, PM, join to knit in the round.

Round 1: [Kfb] 4 times. (8 sts)

Round 2: [Kfb] 8 times. (16 sts)

Round 3: Knit.

Divide sts evenly between 4 DPNs, 4 per needle.

Round 4: [K1, m1, k2, m1, k1] 4 times. (24 sts)

Rounds 5-6: Knit.

Round 7: [K2, m1, k2, m1, k2] 4 times. (32 sts)

Rounds 8–9: Knit.

Round 10: [K3, m1, knit to last 3 sts on DPN, m1, k3] 4 times. (40 sts)

Repeat rounds 8–10 once more until you have 48 sts, 12 on each needle.

Rounds 14–15: Knit.

Round 16: [K3, m1, k6, m1, k15] twice. (52 sts)

Rounds 17–18: Knit.

Round 19: [K3, m1, k8, m1, k15] twice. (56 sts)

Rounds 20–21: Knit.

Round 22: [K3, m1, k10, m1, k15] twice. (60 sts)

Rounds 23–30: Knit.

Round 31: [K3, k2tog, k8, k2tog, k15] twice. (56 sts)

Round 32: Knit.

Round 33: [K3, k2tog, k6, k2tog, k15] twice. (52 sts)

Round 34: Knit.

Round 35: [K3, k2tog, k4, k2tog, k15] twice. (48 sts)

Round 36: Knit.

Round 37: [K3, k2tog, k2, k2tog, k3] 4 times. (40 sts)

Round 38: Knit.

Round 39: [K2, k2tog, k2, k2tog, k2] 4 times. (32 sts)

Round 40: Knit.

BO. Stuff head firmly.

FACE TRIM

Using US 5 (3.75mm) DPNs and **B**, pick up and knit 21 sts along base of head centered where chin will be.

Row 1: Kfb, knit to last 2 sts, kfb, k1. (23 sts)

Row 2: Purl.

Repeat rows 1–2 three more time. (29 sts)

Row 9: K1, k2tog, knit to last 3 sts, k2tog, k1. (27 sts)

Row 10: Purl.

Row 11: Knit.

Row 12: Purl.

Row 13: K1, k2tog, knit to last 3 sts, k2tog, k1. (25 sts)

Row 14: P1, p2tog, purl to last 3 sts, p2tog, p1. (23 sts)

Row 15: BO 3 sts, knit to end. (20 sts)

Row 16: BO 3 sts, purl to end. (17 sts)

Rows 17–20: Work in st st.

Row 21: K1, k2tog, k11, k2tog, k1. (15 sts)

Row 22: Purl.

Row 23: K1, k2tog, k4, BO 1 st (1 st left on right needle after BO), k3, k2tog, k1. (12 sts)

BO two sets of 6 sts separately.

BODY

Using US 5 (3.75mm) DPNs and **A**, CO 4 sts, PM, join to knit in the round.

Round 1: [Kfb] 4 times. (8 sts)

Round 2: [Kfb] 8 times. (16 sts)

Round 3: Knit.

Divide sts evenly between 4 DPNs, 4 per needle.

Round 4: [K1, m1, k2, m1, k1] 4 times. (24 sts)

Round 5: Knit.

Round 6: [K2, m1, k2, m1, k2] 4 times. (32 sts)

Round 7: Knit.

Round 8: [K3, m1, knit to last 3 sts on DPN, m1, k3] 4 times. (40 sts)

Repeat rounds 7–8 three more times, until you have 64 sts, 16 on each needle.

Rounds 15–20: Knit.

Round 21: [K3, k2tog, knit to last 5 sts on needle, k2tog, k3] 4 times. (56 sts)

Round 22: Knit.

Repeat rounds 21–22 three more times, until you have 32 sts, 8 on each needle.

Round 29: [K2, k2tog, k2tog, k2] 4 times. (24 sts)

HEAD

FACE TRIM

BODY

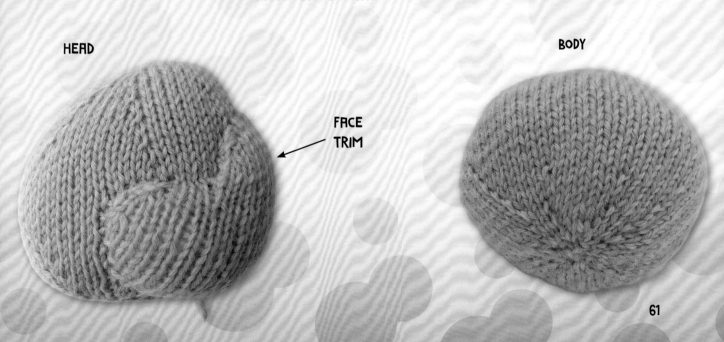

PROJECT 11 / TURTWIG

Round 30: Knit.

Stuff body.

Round 31: [K1, k2tog twice. k1] 4 times. (16 sts)

Round 32: Knit.

Round 33: [K2tog] 8 times. (8 sts)

Round 34: [K2tog] 4 times. (4 sts)

Break yarn, pull tail through remaining sts. Weave in loose ends.

LEGS (make 4)

Using US 5 (3.75mm) DPNs and **A**, CO 4 sts, PM, join to knit in the round.

Round 1: [Kfb] 4 times. (8 sts)

Round 2: [Kfb] 8 times. (16 sts)

Round 3: [K1, kfb, k2] 4 times. (20 sts)

Rounds 4–8: Knit.

Round 9: K15, BO5. (15 sts)

Row 10: Knit to last 2 sts, k2tog. (14 sts)

Row 11: Purl to last 2 sts, p2tog. (13 sts)

Repeat rows 10–11 twice more until you have 9 sts.

Row 16: K1, k2tog, k3, k2tog, k1. (7 sts)

Row 17: Purl.

Row 18: K1, k2tog, k1, k2tog, k1. (5 sts)

BO purlwise.

LEG TRIM (make 4)

Using US 5 (3.75mm) DPNs and **B**, CO 4 sts, PM, join to knit in the round.

Round 1: [Kfb] 4 times. (8 sts)

Round 2: [Kfb] 8 times. (16 sts)

Round 3: Knit.

Round 4: [K1, m1, k2, m1, k1] 4 times. (24 sts)

Rounds 5–6: Knit.

Divide for edge triangles:

Row 1: K2, k2tog, k2, turn.

Continue knitting these 5 sts in rows.

Row 2: Purl.

Row 3: K1, k2tog, k2. (4 sts)

Row 4: P2tog twice. (2 sts)

Break yarn, pull tail through remaining sts. Weave in loose ends.

Reattach yarn and repeat rows 1–4 a further three times for the remaining sts.

TAIL

Using US 5 (3.75mm) DPNs and **A**, CO 14 sts.

Round 1: Knit.

Round 2: K2tog, k10, k2tog. (12 sts)

Round 3: Knit.

Round 4: K2tog, k8, k2tog. (10 sts)

Round 5: Knit.

Round 6: [K2tog, k1, k2tog] twice. (6 sts)

Round 7: [K2tog] 3 times. (3 sts)

Break yarn, pull tail through remaining sts. Weave in loose ends.

SHELL

Using US 5 (3.75mm) DPNs and **C**, CO 4 sts, PM, join to knit in the round.

Round 1: [Kfb] 4 times. (8 sts)

Round 2: [Kfb] 8 times. (16 sts)

Round 3: Knit.

Divide sts evenly between 4 DPNs, 4 per needle.

Round 4: [K1, m1, k2, m1, k1] 4 times. (24 sts)

Round 5: Knit.

Round 6: [K2, m1, k2, m1, k2] 4 times. (32 sts)

Round 7: Knit.

Round 8: [K3, m1, knit to last 3 sts on DPN, m1, k3] 4 times. (40 sts)

Repeat rounds 7–8 three more times, until you have 64 sts, 16 on each needle.

Rounds 15–20: Knit.

BO.

SHELL TRIM (make 2)

Using US 5 (3.75mm) DPNs and **D**, CO 6 sts, PM, join to knit in the round.

Work in st st until piece measures 10½in (27cm). BO.

Work in st st on the second piece until it measures 14¾in (37.5cm).

HAT

Using US 5 (3.75mm) DPNs and **C**, CO 1 st.

Row 1 (RS): Kfb. (2 sts)

Row 2: Pfb, p1. (3 sts)

Row 3: Knit.

Row 4: [Pfb] twice, p1. (5 sts)

Row 5: Knit.

Break yarn. Leave sts on a piece of scrap yarn or DPN.

Repeat rows 1–5 four more times to create 5 total triangles.

Connect pieces:

Reconnect **C**, and knit across the 5 sts from the first triangle, *knit across the 5 sts from the next triangle, repeat from * for remaining triangles, dividing sts over 3 DPNs, PM, join to knit in the round. (25 sts)

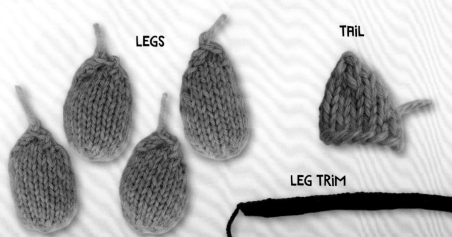

LEGS

TAIL

LEG TRIM

62

Round 1: [K2, k2tog, k1] 5 times. (20 sts)

Round 2: [K1, k2tog, k1] 5 times. (15 sts)

Round 3: [K1, k2tog] 5 times. (10 sts)

Round 4: [K2, k2tog, k1] twice. (8 sts)

Rounds 5–6: Knit.

Round 7: [K1, k2tog, k1] twice. (6 sts)

Rounds 8–9: Knit.

Round 10: [K1, k2tog] twice. (4 sts)

Rounds 11–12: Knit.

Round 13: [K2tog] twice. (2 sts)

Break yarn, pull tail through remaining sts. Weave in loose ends.

ASSEMBLY

Cut out all felt pieces using templates.

Use images as guides for positioning.

Glue felt pieces for eyes.

Sew head trim to bottom of head, centering cheeks halfway up each side, stuffing lightly as you go.

Sew hat to top of head.

Sew leg trim to legs.

Sew legs to bottom of body.

Sew shell to body.

Sew shorter length of shell trim in a band around bottom of shell.

Sew longer length of shell trim over the top of the shell, centering ends in the middle.

Sew head to body

Sew tail to body.

Use green embroidery thread to secure leaves to side of hat.

Use black embroidery thread to embroider nostrils.

Be sure to weave in all ends to ensure a smooth finish.

SHELL TRIM

SHELL

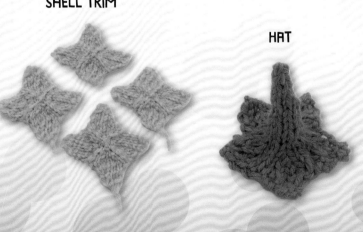

HAT

BULBASAUR

OFFICIAL COLORS

NATIONAL POKÉDEX NO.	TYPE	WEIGHT	HEIGHT
0001	Grass/ Poison	15.2 lbs/ 6.9 kg	2 ft 4 in/ 0.7 m

For some time after its birth, it uses the nutrients that are packed into the seed on its back in order to grow.

MATERIALS

- Cascade 220 (100% wool), 10 ply/ aran, 100g (220yd/200m), in the following shades:
- Aqua Haze (9634); 1 ball (**A**)
- Fern Heather (1035); 1 ball (**B**)
- Black (8555); 20yd/18m (**C**)
- Fingering weight yarn; White oddments (**D**)
- Set of 5 size US 5 (3.75mm) DPNs
- Set of 2 size US 1 (2.25mm) DPNs
- Felt scraps in black, white, blue, and red
- Felt glue
- Polyester filling

GAUGE

22 sts and 26 rows measure 4 x 4in (10 x 10cm) over stockinette stitch (stocking stitch) using US 5 (3.75mm) needles.

FINISHED SIZE

7in (18cm) long

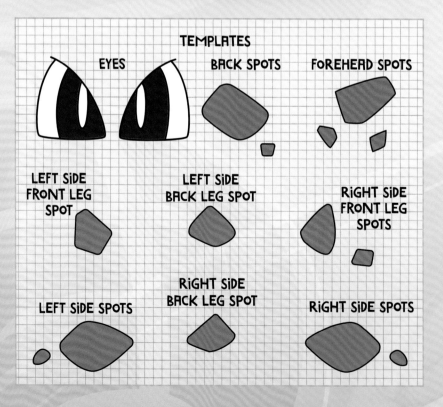

TEMPLATES

EYES   BACK SPOTS   FOREHEAD SPOTS

LEFT SIDE FRONT LEG SPOT   LEFT SIDE BACK LEG SPOT   RIGHT SIDE FRONT LEG SPOTS

RIGHT SIDE BACK LEG SPOT

LEFT SIDE SPOTS   RIGHT SIDE SPOTS

BULB

Using US 5 (3.75mm) DPNs and B CO 6 sts, PM, join to knit in the round.

Round 1: [Kfb] 6 times. (12 sts)

Round 2: [Kfb, k1] 6 times. (18 sts)

Round 3: [Kfb, k2] 6 times. (24 sts)

Round 4: [P1, k2, p1] 6 times.

Round 5: [P1, m1, k2, m1, p1] 6 times. (36 sts)

Round 6: [P1, k4, p1] 6 times.

Round 7: [P1, k1, m1, k2, m1, k1, p1] 6 times. (48 sts)

Round 8: [P1, k6, p1] 6 times.

Round 9: [P1, k2, m1, k1, m1, k1, m1, k2, p1] 6 times. (66 sts)

Round 10: [P1, k9, p1] 6 times.

Round 11: [P1, k3, m1, k3, m1, k3, p1] 6 times. (78 sts)

Rounds 12–15: [P1, k11, p1] 6 times.

Round 16: [P1, k1, k2tog, k5, k2tog, k1, p1] 6 times. (66 sts)

Rounds 17–20: [P1, k9, p1] 6 times.

Round 21: [P1, K1, k2tog, k1, k2tog, k1, k2tog, p1] 6 times. (48 sts)

Rounds 22–25: [P1, k6, p1] 6 times.

Round 26: [P1, k2tog, k2, k2tog, p1] 6 times. (36 sts)

Rounds 27–29: [P1, k4, p1] 6 times.

Round 30: [P1, k2tog twice, p1] 6 times. (24 sts)

Stuff bulb.

Round 31: [P1, k2tog, (p2tog, k2tog) 5 times, pirl together the last st of round with first st of round, removing marker and replacing after decreased st]. (12 sts)

Rounds 32–34: [K1, p1] 6 times.
BO. Use tail to gently close hole at top.

BODY AND HEAD
(worked from tail to nose)

Using US 5 (3.75mm) DPNs and **A**, CO 4 sts, PM, join to knit in the round.

Round 1: [Kfb] 4 ttimes. (8 sts)

Round 2: [Kfb] 8 times. (16 sts)

Divide sts evenly between 4 dpns, 4 sts on each needle.

Round 3: Knit.

Round 4: [K1, m1, k2, m1, k1] 4 times. (24 sts)

Round 5: Knit.

Round 6: [K2, m1, knit to last 2 sts on current needle, m1, k2] 4 times. (32 sts)

Repeat rounds 5–6 until you have 48 sts, 12 on each needle.

Rounds 11–29: Knit.

Round 30: K1, k2tog, k8, m1, k14, m1, k8, k2tog, k13.

Round 31: Knit.

Repeat rounds 30–31 four more times.

Rounds 40–46: Knit.

Stuff body.

Round 47: K9, k2tog, k14, k2tog, k21. (46 sts)

Round 48: Knit.

Round 49: K8, k2tog, k2, k2tog, k6, k2tog, k2, k2tog, k9, k2tog, k6, k2tog, k1. (40 sts)

Round 50: Knit.

Round 51: K7, k2tog, k12, k2tog, k17. (38 sts)

Round 52: Knit.

Round 53: K6, k2tog, k2, k2tog, k4, k2tog, k2, k2tog, k7, k2tog, k4, k2tog, k1. (32 sts)

Round 54: Knit.

Round 55: K5, k2tog, k10, k2tog, k13. (30 sts)

Round 56: Knit.

Round 57: K4, k2tog, k2, k2tog, k2, k2tog, k2, k2tog, k5, k2tog, k2, k2tog, k1. (24 sts)

Round 58: Knit.

Stuff head.

Round 59: [K2tog] 12 times. (12 sts)

Round 60: [K2tog] 6 times. (6 sts)

Break yarn, weave loose end through remaining sts, knot, pull knot to inside of fabric to secure.

BULB

BODY AND HEAD

PROJECT 12 / BULBASAUR

BACK LEGS (make 2)

Using US 5 (3.75mm) DPNs and **A**, CO 4 sts, PM, join to knit in the round.

Round 1: [Kfb] 4 times. (8 sts)

Round 2: [Kfb] 8 times. (16 sts)

Round 3: [Kfb, k3] 4 times. (20 sts)

Rounds 4–5: Knit.

Round 6: BO 5 sts (1 st left on RN), k12, k2tog. (14 sts)

Turn and continue knitting in rows.

Row 7: Purl to last 2 sts, p2tog. (13 sts)

Row 8: Knit to last 2 sts, k2tog. (12 sts)

Repeat rows 7–8 until 6 sts remain.

BO, leaving long tail for seaming.

Stuff legs.

FRONT LEGS (make 2)

Using US 5 (3.75mm) DPNs and **A**, CO 4 sts, PM, join to knit in the round.

Round 1: [Kfb] 4 times. (8 sts)

Round 2: [Kfb] 8 times. (16 sts)

Round 3: [Kfb, k3] 4 times. (20 sts)

Rounds 4–8: Knit.

Round 9: BO 5 sts, (1 st left on RN), k12, k2tog. (14 sts)

Turn and continue knitting in rows

Row 10: Purl to last 2 sts, p2tog. (13 sts)

Row 11: Knit to last 2 sts, k2tog. (12 sts)

Repeat rows 10–11 until 6 sts remain. BO, leaving long tail for seaming.

Stuff legs.

EARS (make 2)

Using US 5 (3.75mm) DPNs and **A**, CO 12 sts, PM, join to knit in the round.

Round 1: Knit.

Round 2: [K2tog, k2] 3 times. (9 sts)

Round 3: Knit.

Round 4: [K2tog, k1] 3 times. (6 sts)

Round 5: [K2tog] 3 times. (3 sts)

Break yarn, weave loose end through remaining sts, knot, pull knot to inside of fabric to secure.

Stuff ears.

CLAWS (make 12—complete after seaming legs to body)

Using US 1 (2.25mm) DPNs and **D**, pick up and knit 2 sts from the center front bottom edge of each leg which makes the foot.

Complete 1 round of i-cord.

Break yarn, weave loose end through remaining sts, knot, pull knot to inside of fabric to secure.

Repeat once on each side of the center claw, spaced about ¼in (0.5cm) apart, to make 3 claws on each foot.

ASSEMBLY

Cut out all felt pieces using templates, using images as guides for positioning.

Sew legs to body.

Sew ears to body.

Sew bulb to body.

Glue eyes and spots into place.

Knit claws onto front edge of feet.

Use **C** to embroider mouth and nostrils.

Use **C** to outline tops and bottoms of eyes and to create eyebrows.

Weave in all ends to ensure a smooth finish.

BACK LEGS   FRONT LEGS   EARS

EEVEE

OFFICIAL COLORS

NATIONAL POKÉDEX NO.	TYPE	WEIGHT	HEIGHT
0133	Normal	14.3 lbs/ 6.5 kg	1 ft 0 in/ 0.3 m

Its ability to evolve into many forms allows Eevee to adapt smoothly and perfectly to any environment.

MATERIALS

- Cascade 220 (100% wool), 10 to ply/aran, 100g (220yd/200m), in the following shades:
- Sunflower (2415); 1 ball (**A**)
- Antiqued heather (9600); 100yds/91m (**B**)
- Black (8555); 20yd/18m (**C**)
- Set of five size 3.75mm (US 5) DPNs
- Felt pieces in black, white, light brown, dark brown, and pink
- Fabric glue
- Polyester filling
- Small crochet hook
- Brush

GAUGE
22 sts and 26 rows measure 4 x 4in (10 x 10cm) over stockinette stitch (stocking stitch) using 3.75mm (US 5)

FINISHED SIZE
12in (30cm) long

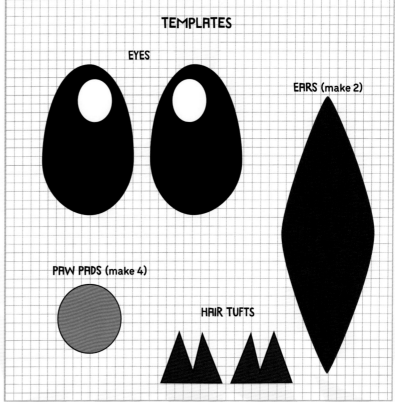

TEMPLATES

EYES

EARS (make 2)

PAW PADS (make 4)

HAIR TUFTS

BODY

Using US 5 (3.75mm) DPNs and **A**, CO 4 sts, PM, join to knit in the round.

Round 1: [Kfb] 4 times. (8 sts)

Round 2: [Kfb] 8 times. (16 sts)

Round 3: Knit.

Round 4: [K1, m1, k2, m1, k1] 4 times. (24 sts)

Round 5: Knit.

Round 6: [K2, m1, k2, m1, k2] 4 times. (32 sts)

Round 7: Knit.

Round 8: [K3, m1, k2, m1, k3] 4 times. (40 sts)

Rounds 9–10: Knit.

Round 11: [K3, m1, k4, m1, k3] 4 times. (48 sts)

Rounds 12–42: Knit.

Round 43: [K3, k2tog, k2, k2tog, k3] 4 times. (40 sts)

Rounds 44–45: Knit.

Stuff body.

Round 46: [K2, k2tog, k2, k2tog, k2] 4 times. (32 sts)

Round 47: Knit.

Round 48: [K1, k2tog, k2, k2tog, k1] 4 times. (24 sts)

Round 49: Knit.

Round 50: [K1, k2tog, k2tog, k1] 4 times. (16 sts)

Round 51: Knit.

Stuff remainder of body.

Round 52: [K2tog] 8 times. (8 sts)

Round 53: [K2tog] 4 times. (4 sts)

Break yarn, pull tail through remaining sts, knot, and pull knot to inside of fabric.

HEAD

Using US 5 (3.75mm) DPNs and **A**, CO 4 sts, PM, join to knit in the round.

Round 1: [Kfb] 4 times. (8 sts)

Round 2: [Kfb] 8 times. (16 sts)

Round 3: Knit.

Round 4: [K1, m1, k2, m1, k1] 4 times. (24 sts)

Round 5: Knit.

Round 6: [K2, m1, k2, m1, k2] 4 times. (32 sts)

Round 7: Knit

Round 8: [K3, m1, k2, m1, k3] 4 times. (40 sts)

Rounds 9–11: Repeat rounds 7–8 twice more, until you have 56 sts, 14 on each needle.

Rounds 13–37: Knit.

Round 38: [K3, k2tog, knit to last 5 sts on current needle, k2tog, k3] 4 times. (48 sts)

Round 39: Knit.

Round 40: [K3, k2tog, knit to last 5 sts on current needle, k2tog, k3] 4 times. (40 sts)

Round 41: Knit.

Round 42: [K2, k2tog, knit to last 5 sts on current needle, k2tog, k2] 4 times. (32 sts)

BO. Stuff head.

TAIL

Using US 5 (3.75mm) DPNs and **A**, CO 24 sts, PM, join to knit in the round.

Divide sts evenly across 4 DPNs, 6 sts per needle.

Round 1: Knit.

Round 2: [K2, m1, knit to last 2 sts on current needle, m1, k2] 4 times. (32 sts)

Round 3: Knit.

Round 4: [K3, m1, knit to last 2 sts on current needle, m1, k3] 4 times. (40 sts)

Rounds 5–8: Repeat rounds 3 and 4 twice more until you have 56 sts, 14 on each needle.

Rounds 9–16: Knit.

Round 17: [K2, k2tog, knit to last 4 sts on current needle, k2tog, k2] 4 times. (48 sts)

Rounds 18–24: Knit.

Rounds 25–32: Repeat rounds 17 to 24 once more until you have 40 sts remaining.

Round 33: [K2, k2tog, knit to last 4 sts on current needle, k2tog, k2] 4 times. (32 sts)

Join in **B**.

Round 34: [K1 in **B**, k3 in **A**] 8 times.

Round 35: [K2 in **B**, k1 in **A**, k1 in **B**] 8 times.

Break **A**. Continue with **B** only.

Rounds 36 to 40: Knit.

Round 41: [K1, k2tog, knit to last 3 sts on current needle, k2tog, k1] 4 times. (24 sts)

Round 42 to 45: Knit.

Round 46: [K2, k2tog, k2] 4 times. (20 sts)

Round 47–48: Knit.

Round 49: [K2tog, k3] 4 times. (16 sts)

Round 50–51: Knit.

Round 52: [K2tog] 8 times. (8 sts)

Round 53: Knit.

Round 54: [K2tog] 4 times. (4 sts)

Break yarn, pull tail through remaining sts, knot, and pull knot to inside of fabric. Stuff tail.

BODY

TAIL

HEAD

PROJECT 13 / EEVEE

FRONT LEGS (make 2)

Using US 5 (3.75mm) DPNs and **A**, CO 4 sts, PM, join to knit in the round.

Round 1: [Kfb] 4 times. (8 sts)

Round 2: [Kfb] 8 times. (16 sts)

Round 3: [K2, m1, k2] 4 times. (20 sts)

Round 4: [K1, m1, k3, m1, k6] twice. (24 sts)

Rounds 5–7: Knit.

Round 8: K5, k2tog, k5, k2tog, knit to end. (22 sts)

Round 9: K4, k2tog, k5, k2tog, knit to end. (20 sts)

Round 10: Knit.

Round 11: K1, m1, k1, k2tog, k7, k2tog, k1, m1, knit to end.

Rounds 12–14: Knit.

Round 15: K1, m1, k1, k2tog, k7, k2tog, k1, m1, knit to end.

Round 16: Knit.

Round 17: K1, k2tog, k1, m1, k7, m1, k1, k2tog, knit to end.

Rounds 18–19: Knit.

Round 20: K1, k2tog, k1, m1, k7, m1, k1, k2tog, knit to end.

Round 21: Knit.

Begin upper portion of leg.

Right leg

Round 22: BO 5 sts, knit to last 2 sts, k2tog. (14 sts)

Turn and continue knitting in rows.

Row 23: Purl to last 2 sts, p2tog. (13 sts)

Row 24: Knit to last 2 sts, k2tog. (12 sts)

Rows 25 onward: Repeat rows 23 and 24 until 6 sts remain.

BO and stuff.

Left leg

Round 22: K10, BO 5 sts, return st on right needle after BO to left needle, k2tog, k3, remove marker. (14 sts)

Turn and continue knitting in rows.

Row 23: Knit to last 2 sts, k2tog. (13 sts)

Row 24: Purl to last 2 sts, p2tog. (12 sts)

Rows 25 onward: Repeat rows 23 and 24 until 5 sts remain.

BO and stuff.

BACK LEGS (make 2)

Using US 5 (3.75mm) DPNs and **A**, CO 4 sts, PM, join to knit in the round.

Round 1: [Kfb] 4 times. (8 sts)

Round 2: [Kfb] 8 times. (16 sts)

Round 3: [K2, m1, k2] 4 times. (20 sts)

Round 4: [K1, m1, k3, m1, k6] twice. (24 sts)

Rounds 5–7: Knit.

Round 8: K5, k2tog, k5, k2tog, knit to end. (22 sts)

Round 9: K4, k2tog, k5, k2tog, knit to end. (20 sts)

Round 10: Knit.

Round 11: K1, m1, k1, k2tog, k7, k2tog, k1, m1, knit to end.

Rounds 12–14: Knit.

Round 15: K1, m1, k1, k2tog, k7, k2tog, k1, m1, knit to end.

Rounds 16: Knit.

Round 21: K4, m1, k7, m1, knit to end. (22 sts)

Round 22: Knit.

Round 23: K1, k2tog, k2, m1, k7, m1, k2, k2tog, knit to end.

Round 24: Knit.

Round 25: K5, m1, k7, m1, knit to end. (24 sts)

Round 26: Knit.

Round 27: K1, k2tog, k3, m1, k7, m1, k3, k2tog, knit to end.

Round 28: Knit.

Round 29: K6, m1, k7, m1, knit to end. (26 sts)

Begin upper portion of leg.

Right leg

Round 30: BO 8 sts, knit to last 2 sts, k2tog. (17 sts)

Turn and continue knitting in rows.

Row 31: P5, p2tog, p4, m1, p4, p2tog. (16 sts)

Row 32: Knit to last 2 sts, k2tog. (15 sts)

Row 33: P10, m1, p3, p2tog.

Row 34: Knit to last 2 sts, k2tog. (14 sts)

Row 35: P3, p2tog, p5, m1, p2, p2tog. (13 sts)

Row 36: Knit to last 2 sts, k2tog. (12 sts)

Row 37: P9, m1, p1, p2tog.

Row 38: K1, k2tog, k6, k2tog, k1. (10 sts)

FRONT LEGS

BACK LEGS

EARS

Row 39: Purl.

Row 40: K1, k2tog, k4, k2tog, k1. (8 sts)

Row 41: P1, p2tog, p2, p2tog, p1. (6 sts)
BO and stuff.

Left leg

Round 30: K13, BO 8 sts, return st on right needle after BO to left needle, k2tog, k3. (17 sts)

Remove marker, turn and continue knitting in rows.

Row 31: K1, k2tog, k4, m1, k4, k2tog. (16 sts)

Row 32: Purl to last 2 sts, p2tog. (15 sts)

Row 33: K10, m1, k3, k2tog.

Row 34: Purl to last 2 sts, p2tog. (14 sts)

Row 35: K3, k2tog, k5, m1, k2, k2tog. (13 sts)

Row 36: Purl to last 2 sts, p2tog. (12 sts)

Row 37: K9, m1, k1, k2tog.

Row 38: P1, p2tog, purl to last 3 sts, p2tog, p1. (10 sts)

Row 39: Knit.

Row 40: P1, p2tog, p4, p2tog, p1. (8 sts)

Row 41: K1, k2tog, k2, k2tog, k1. (6 sts)
BO and stuff.

EARS (make 2)

Using US 5 (3.75mm) DPNs and **A**, CO 10 sts, PM, join to knit in the round.

Divide sts evenly between 2 DPNs, 5 sts per needle.

Rounds 1–3: Knit.

Round 4: [K1, m1, knit to last st on current needle, m1, k1] twice. (14 sts)

Rounds 5 to 8: Knit.

Round 9: [K1, m1, knit to last st on current needle, m1, k1] twice. (18 sts)

Rounds 10–12: Knit.

Round 13: [K1, m1, knit to last st on current needle, m1, k1] twice. (22 sts)

Rounds 14–17: Knit.

Round 18: [K1, m1, knit to last st on current needle, m1, k1] twice. (26 sts)

Round 19: Knit.

Round 20: [K1, k2tog, knit to last 3 sts on current needle, k2tog, k1] twice. (22 sts)

Rounds 21–23: Knit.

Rounds 24 to 31: Repeat rounds 20–23 until you have 14 sts, 7 on each needle.

Round 32: [K1, k2tog, knit to last 3 sts on current needle, k2tog, k1] twice. (10 sts)

Round 33: Knit.

Round 34: [K2tog, k1, k2tog] twice. (6 sts)

Round 35: [K2tog] 3 times. (3 sts)

Break yarn, pull tail through remaining sts, knot, and pull knot to inside of fabric.

Stuff ears lightly.

ASSEMBLY

Cut out all felt pieces using templates.

Use images as guides for positioning.

Glue eyes to face.

Glue inner ear and hair tufts to ears.

Glue paw pads to feet as shown (see figure 1 below).

Embroider mouth and nose using yarn **C**.

Sew head to body.

Sew legs to body.

Sew tail to body.

Sew ears to head.

Cut several 4in (10cm) strands of yarn **B**. Working one strand at a time, use the crochet hook to attach each strand around the base of the head, brushing them out with a toothbrush or felt brush as you go. Once the mane is full enough, trim into shape using the images as a guide.

Be sure to weave in all ends to ensure a smooth finish.

figure 1

SLOWPOKE

OFFICIAL COLORS

NATIONAL POKÉDEX NO.	TYPE	WEIGHT	HEIGHT
0079	Water/ Psychic	79.4 lbs/ 36.0 kg	3 ft 11 in/ 1.2 m

It is always vacantly lost in thought, but no one knows what it is thinking about. It is good at fishing with its tail.

MATERIALS

- Cascade 220 (100% wool), 10-ply/ aran, 100g (220yd/200m), in the following shades:

- Peony (1057); 1 ball (**A**)

- Antiqued Heather (9600); 110yd/100m (**B**)

- White (8505); Oddments (**C**)

- Black (8555); Oddments (**D**)

- White fingering yarn; Oddments (**E**)

- Set of five size US 5 (3.75mm) DPNs

- Set of five size US 2 (2.75mm) DPNs

- Felt pieces in black and white

- Fabric glue

- Polyester filling

GAUGE

22 sts and 26 rows measure 4 x 4in (10 x 10cm) over stockinette stitch (stocking stitch) using size US 5 (3.75mm) needles.

FINISHED SIZE

10in (25.5cm) long

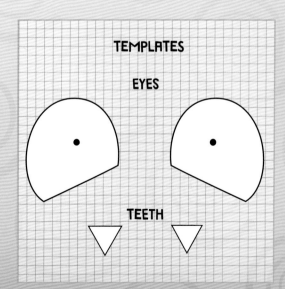

TEMPLATES

EYES

TEETH

HEAD AND BODY

(worked from nose to tail)

Using US 5 (3.75mm) DPNs and **A**, CO 4 sts, PM, join to knit in the round.

Round 1: [Kfb] 4 times. (8 sts)

Round 2: [Kfb] 8 times. (16 sts)

Round 3: Knit.

Divide sts evenly between 4 DPNs, 4 sts per needle.

Round 4: [K1, m1, k2, m1, k1] 4 times. (24 sts)

Round 5: Knit.

Round 6: [K2, m1, k2, m1, k2] 4 times. (32 sts)

Round 7: Knit

Round 8: [K3, m1, knit to last 3 sts on DPN, m1, k3] 4 times. (40 sts)

Round 9: Knit.

Round 10: [K13, m1, k4, m1, k5] twice. (44 sts)

Round 11: Knit.

Round 12: [K13, m1, k6, m1, k3] twice. (48 sts)

Rounds 13–22: Knit.

Cut a 10in (26cm) strand of yarn **A**. Without removing sts from needles, thread the yarn through the stitches. Secure loose ends together and drop end of strand into inside of toy. This anchor line with help the neck and head hold shape while stuffing.

Stuff head.

Round 23: K9, m1, k4, m1, k8, m1, k4, m1, k12, m1, k8, m1, k3. (54 sts)

Rounds 24–26: Knit.

Round 27: K10, m1, k4, m1, k10, m1, k4, m1, k13, m1, k10, m1, k3. (60 sts)

Rounds 28–30: Knit.

Round 31: K11, m1, k4, m1, k12, m1, k4, m1, k14, m1, k12, m1, k3. (66 sts)

Rounds 32–34: Knit.

Round 35: K12, m1, k4, m1, k14, m1, k4, m1, k15, m1, k14, m1, k3. (72 sts)

Rounds 36–38: Knit.

Round 39: K13, m1, k4, m1, k16, m1, k4, m1, k16, m1, k16, m1, k3. (78 sts)

Rounds 40–54: Knit.

Round 55: [K18, k2tog, k14, k2tog, k3] twice. (74 sts)

Rounds 56–57: Knit.

Round 58: [K18, k2tog, k12, k2tog, k3] twice. (70 sts)

Round 59: Knit.

Round 60: [K18, k2tog, k10, k2tog, k3] twice. (66 sts)

Round 61: Knit.

Round 62: [K18, k2tog, k8, k2tog, k3] twice. (62 sts)

Round 63: Knit.

Round 64: K12, k2tog, k4, k2tog, k6, k2tog, k4, k2tog, k15, k2tog, k6, k2tog, k3. (56 sts)

Round 65: Knit.

Round 66: [K3, k2tog, k4, k2tog, k3] 4 times. (48 sts)

Round 67: Knit.

Round 68: [K3, k2tog, k2, k2tog, k3] 4 times. (40 sts)

Round 69: Knit.

Stuff body.

Round 70: (K2, k2tog, k2, k2tog, k2) 4 times. 32 sts

Round 71: Knit.

Round 72: (K1, k2tog, k2, k2tog, k1) 4 times. 24 sts

Round 73: Knit.

Round 74: K2tog 12 times. 12 sts

Round 75: K2tog 6 times. 6 sts

Break yarn, pull tail through remaining sts, and pull loose end into inside of fabric.

MUZZLE

Using US 5 (3.75mm) DPNs and **B**, CO 4 sts, PM, join to knit in the round.

Round 1: [Kfb] 4 times. (8 sts)

Round 2: [Kfb] 8 times. (16 sts)

Round 3: [K4, kfb, k1, kfb, k1] twice. (20 sts)

Round 4: Knit.

Round 5: [K2, m1, k3, m1, k4, m1, k1] twice. (26 sts)

Round 6: Knit.

Round 7: [K1, m1, k3, m1, k2, m1, k6, m1, k1] twice. (34 sts)

Round 8: Knit.

Round 9: [K1, m1, k5, m1, k2, m1, k8, m1, k1] twice. (42 sts)

Round 10: Knit.

Round 11: K11, m1, k4, m1, k16, wrap and turn. (44 sts)

Round 12: P15, wrap and turn.

Round 13: K13, wrap and turn.

Round 14: P11, wrap and turn.

Round 15: K9, wrap and turn.

HEAD AND BODY

MUZZLE

Round 16: P7, wrap and turn.

Round 17: K5, wrap and turn.

Round 18: P3, wrap and turn.

Round 19: Knit to end, picking up and knitting wraps as you go.

Round 20: K12, wrap and turn.

Repeat rounds/rows 10–19. Slip marker as you work back and forth.

Round 30: Knit to end, picking up and knitting wraps as you go.

Round 31: K15, m1, k2, m1, knit to end. (46 sts)

BO.

TAIL

Using US 5 (3.75mm) DPNs and **A**, CO 36 sts, PM, join to knit in the round.

Rounds 1–2: Knit.

Row 3: K29, wrap and turn.

Row 4: P22, wrap and turn.

Row 5: K16, wrap and turn.

Row 6: P10, wrap and turn.

Row 7: K13, wrap and turn.

Row 8: P16, wrap an turn, knit to marker.

Rounds 9–11: Knit.

Repeat rows/rounds 3–11 twice more.

Round 30: K1, k2tog, k26, wrap and turn, p22, wrap and turn, knit to last 3 sts, k2tog, k1. (34 sts)

Rounds 22–23: Knit.

Round 24: K1, k2tog, k25, wrap and turn, p22, wrap and turn, knit to last 3 sts, k2tog, k1. (32 sts)

Rounds 25–26: Knit.

Round 27: K1, k2tog, k22, wrap and turn, p18, wrap and turn, knit to last 3 sts, k2tog, k1. (30 sts)

Rounds 28–29: Knit.

Round 30: K1, k2tog, k21, wrap and turn, p18, wrap and turn, knit to last 3 sts, k2tog, k1. (28 sts)

Rounds 31–32: Knit.

Round 33: K1, k2tog, k19, wrap and turn, p16, wrap and turn, knit to last 3 sts, k2tog, k1. (26 sts)

Rounds 34–35: Knit.

Round 36: K1, k2tog, k17, wrap and turn, p14, wrap and turn, knit to last 3 sts, k2tog, k1. (24 sts)

Rounds 37–38: Knit.

Round 39: K1, k2tog, k15, wrap and turn, p12, wrap and turn, knit to last 3 sts, k2tog, k1. (22 sts)

Rounds 40–41: Knit.

Round 42: K1, k2tog, k13, wrap and turn, p10, wrap and turn, knit to last 3 sts, k2tog, k1. (20 sts)

Rounds 43–44: Knit.

Round 45: K1, k2tog, k12, wrap and turn, p10, wrap and turn, knit to last 3 sts, k2tog, k1. (18 sts)

Rounds 46–47: Knit.

Round 48: K1, k2tog, k10, wrap and turn, p8, wrap and turn, knit to last 3 sts, k2tog, k1. (16 sts)

Join in **C**. Carry strands not in use on inside of fabric.

Round 49: (K1 in **C**, k3 in **A**) 4 times.

Round 50: (K2 in **A**, k1 in **C**) 5 times, k1 in **A**.

Round 51: K1 in **A**, k2tog in **C**, (continue alternating colors on each st for the remainder of the round) k7, wrap and turn, p8, wrap and turn, knit to last 3 sts, k2tog, k1. (14 sts)

Round 52: [K1 in **A**, k2 in **C**] 4 times, k1 in **A**, k1 in **C**.

Round 53: [K2 in **C**, k1 in **A**] 4 times, k2, in **C**. Break **A**. Continue in **C**.

Round 54: K11, wrap and turn, p8, wrap and turn, knit to end.

Rounds 55–56: Knit.

Round 57: K1, k2tog, k7, wrap and turn, p6, wrap and turn, knit to last 3 sts, k2tog, k1. (12 sts)

Round 58: Knit.

Round 59: [K2tog, k1] twice, [K1, k2tog] twice. (8 sts)

Round 60: Knit.

Round 61: [K2tog] 4 times. (4 sts)

Break yarn, pull tail through remaining sts, and pull loose end into inside of fabric. Press tail and stuff.

LEGS (make 4)

Using US 5 (3.75mm) DPNs and **A**, CO 4 sts, PM, join to knit in the round.

Round 1: [Kfb] 4 times. (8 sts)

Round 2: [Kfb] 8 times. (16 sts)

Rounds 3–4: Knit.

Round 5: [K1, m1, k2, m1, k5] twice. (20 sts)

Rounds 6–7: Knit.

Round 8: BO 6 sts (1 st left on right needle after cast off), k4, m1, k4, m1, k5. (16 sts)

Continue working in rows.

Row 9: P2tog, p12, p2tog. (14 sts)

Row 10: Knit.

Row 11: P2tog, p10, p2tog. (12 sts)

Row 12: K3, m1, k6, m1, k3. (14 sts)

Row 13: P2tog, p10, p2tog. (12 sts)

Row 14: Knit.

Row 15: P2tog, p8, p2tog. (10 sts)

Row 16: K1, k2tog, k4, k2tog, k1. (8 sts)

BO purlwise.

TAIL

LEGS AND TOES

TOES (make 4)

Using US 2 (2.75mm) DPNs and **E**, CO 18 sts, PM, join to knit in the round.

Round 1: Knit.

Round 2: (K2tog, k1) 6 times. (12 sts)

Round 3: Knit.

Round 4: [K2tog] 6 times. (6 sts)

Break yarn, pull tail through remaining sts, and pull loose end into inside of fabric.

EARS (make 2)

Using US 5 (3.75mm) DPNs and **A**, CO14 sts, PM, join to knit in the round.

Round 1: Knit.

Round 2: [K4, m1, k2, m1, k1] twice. (18 sts)

Round 3: Knit.

Round 4: [K4, m1, k4, m1, k1] twice. (22 sts)

Round 5: Knit.

Round 6: [K4, k2tog, k2, k2tog, k1] twice. (18 sts)

Round 7: Knit.

Round 8: [K4, k2tog, twice, k1] twice. (14 sts)

Round 9: [K3, k2tog twice] twice. (10 sts)

Round 10: [K2tog] 5 times. (5 sts)

Break yarn, pull tail through remaining sts, and pull loose end into inside of fabric.

ASSEMBLY

Cut out all felt pieces using templates.

Use images as guides for positioning.

Glue felt pieces for eyes.

Glue felt pieces for teeth.

Sew legs to bottom of body.

Sew toes to front edges of feet.

Sew tail to body.

Sew ears to head.

Pin muzzle to face, and sew into place, stuffing as you go.

Use **D** to embroider mouth and nostrils.

Use **D** to create swirls in ears.

Be sure to weave in all ends to ensure a smooth finish.

EARS

MiMiKYU

OFFICIAL COLORS

NATIONAL POKÉDEX No.	TYPE	WEIGHT	HEIGHT
0778	Ghost/Fairy	1.5 lbs/0.7 kg	8 in/0.2 m

This Pokémon lives in dark places untouched by sunlight. When it appears before humans, it hides itself under a cloth that resembles a Pikachu.

MATERIALS

- Cascade 220 (100% wool), 10-ply/aran, 100g (220yd/200m), in the following shades:

- Pear (8412); 1 ball (**A**)

- Jet (4002); 110yds/100m (**B**)

- Carob Brown (1010); 20yd/18m (**C**)

- Black (8555); Oddments (**D**)

- Set of five size US 5 (3.75mm) DPNs

- Felt pieces in orange

- Felt glue

- Polyester filling

GAUGE

22 sts and 26 rows measure 4 x 4in (10 x 10cm) over stockinette stitch (stocking stitch) using US 5 (3.75mm) needles.

FINISHED SIZE

10in (25.5cm) tall

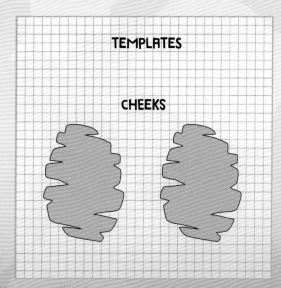

TEMPLATES

CHEEKS

HEAD AND BODY
(worked from the top down)

Using US 5 (3.75mm) DPNs and A, CO 4 sts, PM, join to knit in the round.

Round 1: [Kfb] 4 times. (8 sts)

Round 2: [Kfb] 8 times. (16 sts)

Split sts evenly between 4 DPNs, 4 sts on each needle.

Round 3: Knit.

Round 4: [K1, m1, k2, m1, k1] 4 times. (24 sts)

Round 5: Knit.

Round 6: [K2, m1, k2, m1, k2] 4 times. (32 sts)

Round 7: Knit

Round 8: [K3, m1, knit to last 3 sts, m1, k3] 4 times. (40 sts)

Repeat: Repeat rounds 7–8 twice more, until you have 56 sts, 14 on each needle.

Rounds 13–20: Knit.

Round 21: [K7, m1, k7] 4 times. (60 sts)

Rounds 22–26: Knit.

Round 27: [K8, m1, k7] 4 times. (64 sts)

Rounds 28–30: Knit.

Round 31: [K3, k2tog, knit to last 5 sts on current needle, k2tog, k3] 4 times. (56 sts)

Rounds 32–33: Knit.

Repeat: Repeat rounds 31–33 twice more, until you have 40 sts, 10 on each needle.

Round 40: [K2, k2tog, knit to last 5 sts on current needle, k2tog, k2] 4 times. (32 sts)

Rounds 41–42: Knit.

Round 43: K20, wrap and turn, p16, wrap and turn, knit to end. Pick up and knit wraps together with working stitch as you go.

Round 44: Knit.

Round 45: [K3, m1, knit to last 3 sts on needle, m1, k3] 4 times. (40 sts)

Rounds 46–50: Knit.

Round 51: [K3, m1, knit to last 3 sts on needle, m1, k3] 4 times. (48 sts)

Round 52: K28, wrap and turn, p24, wrap and turn, knit to end. Pick up and knit wraps together with working stitch as you go.

Rounds 53–56: Knit.

Round 57: [K3, m1, knit to last 3 sts on current needle, m1, k3] 4 times. (56 sts)

Rounds 58–62: Knit.

Round 63: [K7, m1, k7] 4 times. (60 sts)

Rounds 64–68: Knit.

Begin shaping for bottom trim:

Row 69: K6, turn, leave remaining sts on separate DPNs or scrap yarn.

Row 70 (WS): K2, k2tog, k2, turn. (5 sts)

Row 71: K2, k2tog, k1. (4 sts)

Row 73: K1, k2tog, k1. (3 sts)

Row 74: S1, k2tog, psso. Break yarn, pull tail through remaining st and weave in loose end.

Reattach working yarn and repeat rows 69–74 nine more times. Lightly press. Stuff head and body.

BASE

Using US 5 (3.75mm) DPNs and B, CO 5 sts, PM, join to knit in the round.

Round 1: [Kfb] 5 times. (10 sts)

Round 2: [Kfb, k1] 5 times. (15 sts)

Round 3: [Kfb, k2] 5 times. (20 sts)

Round 4: [Kfb, k3] 5 times. (25 sts)

Round 5: [Kfb, k4] 5 times. (30 sts)

Round 6: [Kfb, k5] 5 times. (35 sts)

Round 7: Knit.

Round 8: [Kfb, k6] 5 times. (40 sts)

Round 9: Knit.

Round 10: [Kfb, k7] 5 times. (45 sts)

Round 11: Knit.

Round 12: [Kfb, k8] 5 times. (50 sts)

Round 13: Knit.

Round 14: [Kfb, k9] 5 times. (55 sts)

Round 15: Knit.

Round 16: [Kfb, k10] 5 times. (60 sts)

Round 17: Knit.

Divide for trim:

Row 18: K6, turn, leave remaining sts on separate DPNs or scrap yarn.

Row 19: K2, k2tog, k2, turn. (5 sts)

Row 20: K2, k2tog, k1. (4 sts)

Row 21: K1, k2tog, k1. (3 sts)

Row 22: S1, k2tog, psso. Break yarn, pull tail through remaining st and weave in loose end.

Reattach working yarn and repeat rows 18–19 seven more times. 12 sts remain.

Reattach working yarn.

Rows 23–30: Knit.

Divide for back of base:

Row 31: K3, turn. (Keep remaining 9 sts on separate DPN or scrap yarn to be worked later.)

HEAD AND BODY

BASE

Row 32: K3.

Row 33: S1, k2tog, psso. (1 st)

Break yarn, pull tail through remaining st and weave in loose ends.

Place next 6 sts on DPN and reattach working yarn.

Rows 31–34: Knit.

Row 35: K1, [k2tog] twice, k1. (4 sts)

Rows 36–38: Knit.

Row 39: [K2tog] twice. (2 sts)

Break yarn, pull tail through remaining st and weave in loose ends.

Place last 3 sts on DPN and reattach working yarn.

Work rows 31–33 as for beginning of divide for back of base. Weave in loose ends. Lightly press base.

EAR BASE (make 2)

Using US 5 (3.75mm) DPNs and **A**, CO 20 sts, PM, join to knit in the round.

Rounds 1–3: Knit.

Round 4: K7, k2tog, k7, k2tog, k2. (18 sts)

Rounds 5–7: Knit.

Round 8: K6, k2tog, k7, k2tog, k1. (16 sts)

Rounds 9–12: Knit.

Round 13: [K2tog] 8 times. (8 sts)

Round 14: [K2tog] 4 times. (4 sts)

Break yarn, pull tail through remaining sts and weave in loose ends. Stuff.

RIGHT EAR TIP

Using US 5 (3.75mm) DPNs and **B**, CO 8 sts.

Row 1: Kfb, k5, kfb, k1. (10 sts)

Row 2: Purl.

Row 3: Kfb, k7, kfb, k1. (12 sts)

Row 4: Purl.

Row 5: Kfb, k9, kfb, k1. (14 sts)

Divide sts across two DPNs, PM, join to knit in the round.

Round 6: Knit.

Round 7: [K2, k2tog, k3] twice. (12 sts)

Round 8: Knit.

Round 9: K6, wrap and turn, p4, wrap and turn, knit to end.

Round 10: [K2tog, k4] twice. (10 sts)

Rounds 11–15: Knit.

Round 16: K5, wrap and turn, p3, wrap and turn, knit to end,

Round 17: [K3, k2tog] twice. (8 sts)

Rounds 18–19: Knit.

Round 20: [K2tog] 4 times. (4 sts)

Break yarn, pull tail through remaining st and weave in loose ends. Stuff.

LEFT EAR TIP

Using US 5 (3.75mm) DPNs and **B**, CO 3 sts.

Row 1: [Kfb] twice, k1. (5 sts)

Row 2: Purl.

Row 3: Kfb, k2, kfb, k1.(7 sts)

Row 4: Purl.

Break yarn. Set aside DPN with sts. Using another DPN, CO 5 sts, repeat rows 3–4.

Connect base of ear tips

Round 5: Knit across 7 sts on first dpn, then knit across 7 sts on 2nd DPN, PM, join to knit in the round. (14 sts)

Round 6: Knit.

Round 7: [K2tog, k5] twice. (12 sts)

Rounds 8–10: Knit.

Round 11: [K4, k2tog] twice. (10 sts)

Rounds 12–14: Knit.

Round 15: [K2tog, k3] twice. (8 sts)

Rounds 16–17: Knit.

Round 18: [K2tog] 4 times. (4 sts)

Break yarn, pull tail through remaining sts and weave in loose ends. Stuff.

FALSE TAIL

Using US 5 (3.75mm) DPNs and **C**, CO 14 sts, PM, join to knit in the round.

Round 1: Knit.

Round 2: K8, W+Tk.

Round 3: P2, W+Tp.

Round 4: K4, W+Tk.

Round 5: P6, W+Tp.

Round 6: K8, W+Tk.

Round 7: P10, W+Tk, knit to end.

Rounds 8–20: Knit.

Rounds 21–26: Repeat rounds 2–7.

Round 27: [K3, k2tog, k2] twice. (12 sts)

Rounds 28–31: Knit.

Round 32: K1, W+Tk.

Round 33: P2, W+Tp.

Rounds 34–37: Repeat rounds 4–7.

Round 38: [K2, k2tog, k2] twice. (10 sts)

Round 39: Knit.

Round 40: K6, W+Tk.

Rounds 41–43: Repeat rounds 3–5.

Round 44: [K2, k2tog, k1] twice. (8 sts)

Round 45: Knit.

Round 46: K1, W+Tk.

Round 47: P2, W+Tp.

LEFT EAR

RIGHT EAR

FALSE TAIL

Round 48: K4, W+Tk.

Round 49: P6, W+Tp.

Round 50: [K1, k2tog, k1] twice. (6 sts)

Rounds 51–54: Knit. BO.

ASSEMBLY

Cut out all felt pieces using templates.

Use images as guides for positioning.

Seam base to body, so that base triangles show between body triangles and the large section of the base at the back.

Sew ear tips to tops of ears bases.

Sew ears to top of head.

Seam false tail to back of base. Use **C** to tack top to back of head.

Glue felt cheeks to head. Use **D** to create eyes, mouth, marks on front of body, and marks on tail.

Be sure to weave in all ends to ensure a smooth finish.

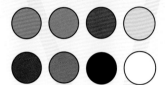

VULPIX

OFFICIAL COLORS

NATIONAL POKÉDEX NO.	TYPE	WEIGHT	HEIGHT
0037	Fire	21.8 lbs/ 9.9 kg	2 ft 0 in/ 0.6 m

If it is attacked by an enemy that is stronger than itself, it feigns injury to fool the enemy and escapes.

MATERIALS

- Cascade 220 (100% wool), 10-ply/ aran, 100g (220yd/200m), in the following shades:
- Jack O Lantern (7824); 1 ball (**A**)
- Burnt Orange (9465B); 1 balll (**B**)
- Pear (8412); 110yd/100m (**C**)
- Ginger (2414); 55yd/50m (**D**)
- Set of five size US5 (3.75mm) DPNs
- Felt pieces in black, white, and tan
- Fabric glue
- Polyester filling

GAUGE

22 sts and 26 rows measure 4 x 4in (10 x 10cm) over stockinette stitch (stocking stitch) using size US 5 (3.75mm) needles.

FINISHED SIZE

10in (25.5cm) tall

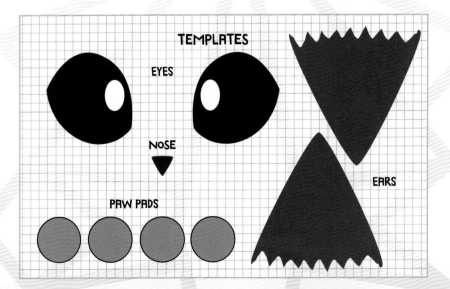

TEMPLATES

EYES

NOSE

PAW PADS

EARS

BODY (worked from tail to neck)

Using US 5 (3.75mm) DPNs and **A**, CO 4 sts, PM, join to knit in the round.

Round 1: [Kfb] 4 times. (8 sts)

Round 2: [Kfb] 8 times. (16 sts)

Round 3: Knit.

Round 4: [K1, m1, k2, m1, k1] 4 times. (24 sts)

Round 5: Knit.

Round 6: [K2, m1, k2, m1, k2] 4 times. (32 sts)

Round 7: Knit

Round 8: [K3, m1, k2, m1, k3] 4 times. (40 sts)

Round 9: Knit.

Round 10: [K3, m1, k4, m1, k3] 4 times. (48 sts)

Rounds 11–29: Knit.

Begin turn for chest:

Row 30: K35, wrap and turn.

Row 31: P34, wrap and turn.

Row 32: K33, wrap and turn.

Row 33: P32, wrap and turn.

Row 34: K31, wrap and turn.

Row 35: P30, wrap and turn.

Row 36: K29, wrap and turn.

Row 37: P28, wrap and turn.

Row 38: K27, wrap and turn.

Row 39: P26, wrap and turn.

Row 40: K25, wrap and turn.

Row 41: P24, wrap and turn.

Row 42: K23, wrap and turn.

Row 43: P22, wrap and turn.

Row 44: K21, wrap and turn.

Row 45: P20, wrap and turn.

Row 46: K19, wrap and turn.

Row 47: P18, wrap and turn.

Row 48: K17, wrap and turn.

Row 49: P16, wrap and turn.

Row 50: K15, wrap and turn.

Row 51: P14, wrap and turn, knit to end.

Pick up and knit in wraps as you go.

Rounds 52–53: Knit.

Round 54: K1, k2tog, k30, k2tog, knit to end. (46 sts)

Round 55: Knit.

Round 56: K1, k2tog, k28, k2tog, knit to end. (44 sts)

Rounds 57–58: Knit.

Round 59: [K12, k2tog, k4, k2tog, k2] twice. (40 sts)

Rounds 60–62: Knit.

Round 63: [K4, k2tog, k4] 4 times. (36 sts) BO. Stuff body.

HEAD

Using US 5 (3.75mm) DPNs and **A**, CO 4 sts, PM, join to knit in the round.

Round 1: [Kfb] 4 times. (8 sts)

Round 2: [Kfb] 8 times. (16 sts)

Round 3: Knit.

Round 4: [K1, m1, k2, m1, k1] 4 times. (24 sts)

Round 5: Knit.

Round 6: [K2, m1, k2, m1, k2] 4 times. (32 sts)

Round 7: Knit

Round 8: [K3, m1, k2, m1, k3] 4 times. (40 sts)

Round 9: Knit.

Round 10: [K3, m1, k4, m1, k3] 4 times. (48 sts)

Rounds 11–12: Knit.

Round 13: [K3, m1, k6, m1, k3] 4 times. (56 sts)

Rounds 14–33: Knit.

Round 34: K11, k2tog, k16, k2tog, knit to end. (54 sts)

Round 35: Knit.

Round 36: K10, k2tog, k16, k2tog, knit to end. (52 sts)

Round 37: Knit.

Round 38: K9, k2tog, k3, k2tog, k6, k2tog, k3, k2tog, k9, k3, k2tog, k6, k2tog, k2. (46 sts)

Round 39: Knit.

Round 40: K8, k2tog, k14, k2tog, knit to end. (44 sts)

Round 41: Knit.

Round 42: K7, k2tog, k14, k2tog, knit to end. (42 sts)

Round 43: Knit.

Round 44: K6, k2tog, k3, k2tog, k4, k2tog, k3, k2tog, k6, k3, k2tog, k4, k2tog, k2. (36 sts)

Round 45: Knit.

Round 46: K5, k2tog, k12, k2tog, knit to end. (34 sts)

Round 47: Knit.

Stuff head.

Round 50: K1, k2tog, k6, k2tog, k2, k2tog, k6, k2tog, k3, k2tog, k2, k2tog, k2. (28 sts)

Round 51: Knit.

Round 52: [K7, k2tog, k2, k2tog, k1] twice. (24 sts)

BODY

HEAD

Round 53: Knit.

Round 54: [K2tog, k1] 8 times. (16 sts)

Round 55: [K2tog] 8 times. (8 sts)

Round 56: [K2tog] 4 times. (4 sts)

Stuff remainder of head. Break yarn, pull tail through remaining sts. Weave in loose end.

BELLY

Using US 5 (3.75mm) DPNs and **C**, CO 5 sts.

Row 1 (RS): Kfb, k2, kfb, k1. (7 sts)

Row 2: Purl.

Row 3: K1, m1, k5, m1, k1. (9 sts)

Work in stockinette st until piece measures 7in (18cm).

Next row: K1, k2tog, k3, k2tog, k1. (7 sts)

Next row: K1, k2tog, k1, k2tog, k1. (5 sts)

BO. Leave long tail for seaming. Press piece.

FRONT LEGS (make 2)

Using US 5 (3.75mm) DPNs and **D**, CO 4 sts, PM, join to knit in the round.

Round 1: [Kfb] 4 times. (8 sts)

Round 2: [Kfb] 8 times. (16 sts)

Round 3: Knit.

Round 4: [K1, m1, k2, m1, k3, m1, k2] twice. (22 sts)

Rounds 5–7: Knit.

Round 8: K4, k2tog, k5, k2tog, knit to end. (20 sts)

Round 9: K3, k2tog, k5, k2tog, knit to end. (18 sts)

Rounds 10–15: Knit.

Join in **A**.

Round 16: *K1 in **A**, k1 in **D**, repeat from * to end of round. Break **D**. Continue in **A**.

Rounds 17–27: Knit.

Begin upper portion of leg:

Right leg:

Row 28: BO 4 sts, knit to last 2 sts, k2tog, remove marker, knit to end. (13 sts) Continue knitting in rows.

Row 29: P2tog, purl to end. (12 sts)

Row 30: K2tog, knit to end. (11 sts)

Repeat rows 29–30 until 5 sts remain. BO.

Left leg:

Row 28: K9, BO 4 sts, slip last st on right needle back to left needle, k2tog, k3, remove marker.

Continue knitting in rows. (13 sts)

Row 29: Knit to last 2 sts, k2tog. (12 sts)

Row 30: Purl to last 2 sts, p2tog. (11 sts)

Repeat rows 29–30 until 5 sts remain. BO.

BACK LEGS (make 2)

Using US 5 (3.75mm) DPNs and **D**, CO 4 sts, PM, join to knit in the round.

Round 1: [Kfb] 4 times. (8 sts)

Round 2: [Kfb] 8 times. (16 sts)

Round 3: Knit.

Round 4: [K1, m1, k2, m1, k3, m1, k2] twice. (22 sts)

Rounds 5–7: Knit.

Round 8: K4, k2tog, k5, k2tog, knit to end. (20 sts)

Round 9: K3, k2tog, k5, k2tog, knit to end. (18 sts)

Rounds 10–11: Knit.

Join in **A**.

Round 16: *K1 in **A**, k1 in **D**, repeat from * to end of round. Break **D**. Continue in **A**.

Rounds 13–18: Knit.

Round 19: K2tog, k1, m1, k7, m1, k1, k2tog, knit to end.

Round 20: K2tog, k1, m1, k7, m1, k1, k2tog, knit to end.

Round 21: Knit.

Round 22: [K1, m1, k2, m1, k6] twice. (22 sts)

Round 23: Knit.

Round 24: [K1, m1, k4, m1, k6] twice. (26 sts)

BELLY

FRONT LEGS

BACK LEGS

Round 25: Knit.

Round 26: [K1, m1, k6, m1, k6] twice. (30 sts)

Rounds 27–28: Knit.

Begin upper portion of leg.

Right leg

Row 29: BO 10 sts, knit to last 2 sts, k2tog. Continue knitting in rows. (19 sts)

Row 30: Purl to last 2 sts, p2tog. (18 sts)

Row 31: Knit to last 2 sts, k2tog. (17 sts)

Repeat rows 30–31 until 11 sts remain.

Row 38: Purl to last 2 sts, p2tog. (10 sts)

Row 39: K1, k2tog, k4, k2tog, k1. (8 sts)

Row 40: Purl.

Row 41: K1, k2tog, k2, k2tog, k1. (6 sts) BO.

Left leg

Row 29: K16, BO 10 sts, knit to end, remove marker, k14, k2tog. (19 sts)

Continue knitting in rows.

Row 30: Purl to last 2 sts, p2tog. (18 sts)

Row 31: Knit to last 2 sts, k2tog. (17 sts)

Repeat rows 30–31 until 11 sts remain.

Row 38: Purl to last 2 sts, p2tog. (10 sts)

Row 39: K1, k2tog, k4, k2tog, k1. (8 sts)

Row 40: Purl.

Row 41: K1, k2tog, k2, k2tog, k1. (6 sts) BO.

Stuff all 4 legs.

EARS (make 2)

Using US 5 (3.75mm) DPNs and **A**, CO 30 sts, PM, join to knit in the round.

Rounds 1–2: Knit.

Round 3: K5, k2tog, k2, k2tog, k9, k2tog, k2, k2tog, k4. (26 sts)

Rounds 4–5: Knit.

Round 6: K4, k2tog, k2, k2tog, k7, k2tog, k2, k2tog, k3. (22 sts)

Rounds 7–8: Knit.

Round 9: K3, k2tog, k2, k2tog, k5, k2tog, k2, k2tog, k2. (18 sts)

Rounds 10–11: Knit.

Round 12: K2, k2tog, k2, k2tog, k3, k2tog, k2, k2tog, k1. (14 sts)

Rounds 13–14: Knit.

Round 15: K1, k2tog, k2, k2tog, k1, k2tog, k2, k2tog. (10 sts)

Round 16: Knit.

Round 17: [K2tog, k1, k2tog] twice. (6 sts)

Round 18: [K2tog] 3 times. (3 sts)

Break yarn, pull tail through remaining sts. Weave in loose end.

TAIL (make 6)

Using US 5 (3.75mm) DPNs and **B**, CO 4 sts, PM, join to knit in the round.

Round 1: [Kfb] 4 times. (8 sts)

Round 2: [Kfb] 8 times. (16 sts)

Round 3: Knit.

Round 4: [K1, m1, k2, m1, k1] 4 times. (24 sts)

Round 5: Knit.

Round 6: [K1, m1, k4, m1, k1] 4 times. (32 sts)

Round 7: Knit.

Round 8: [K1, m1, k6, m1, k9] twice. (36 sts)

Round 9: Knit.

Round 10: [K1, m1, k8, m1, k9] twice. (40 sts)

Rounds 11–18: Knit.

Round 19: K9, k2tog, k10, k2tog, knit to end. (38 sts)

Round 20: Knit.

Round 21: K8, k2tog, k10, k2tog, knit to end. (36 sts)

Round 22: Knit.

Round 23: K7, k2tog, k10, k2tog, knit to end. (34 sts)

Round 24: K6, k2tog, k10, k2tog, knit to end. (32 sts)

Round 25: K5, k2tog, k10, k2tog, knit to end. (30 sts)

Round 26: K4, k2tog, k2, k2tog, k2, k2tog, k2, k2tog, k5, k2tog, k2, k2tog, k1. (24 sts)

Rounds 27–30: Knit.

Round 31: K3, k2tog, k3, k2tog, k3, k2tog, k5, k2tog, k2. (20 sts)

Rounds 32–35: Knit.

Round 36: K2, k2tog, k2, k2tog, k3, k2tog, k4, k2tog, k1. (16 sts)

Rounds 37–43: Knit.

BO. Stuff tail. Use **D** and sewing needle to create tail swirl at end of each tail section.

TAIL

EARS

PROJECT 16 / VULPIX

HAIR CURLS (make 3)

Using US 5 (3.75mm) DPNs and **B**, CO 4 sts, PM, join to knit in the round.

Round 1: [Kfb] 4 times. (8 sts)

Round 2: [Kfb] 8 times. (16 sts)

Round 3: [Kfb, k1] 8 times. (24 sts)

Rounds 4–7: Knit.

Round 8: [K1, k2tog, k2tog, k1] 4 times. (16 sts)

Round 9: [K2tog] 8 times. (8 sts)

Round 10: [K2tog] 4 times. (4 sts)

Break yarn. Pull tail through remaining sts. Stuff curl. Pull sts tight and secure.

LONG HAIR FRINGE

Using US 5 (3.75mm) DPNs and **B**, CO 12 sts, PM, join to knit in the round.

Rounds 1–5: Knit.

Round 6: [K2, k2tog, k2] twice. (10 sts)

Round 7: Knit.

Round 8: [K1, k2tog, k2] twice. (8 sts)

Round 9: Knit.

Round 10: [K2tog] 4 times. (4 sts)

Break yarn. Pull tail through remaining sts.

SHORT HAIR FRINGE (make 2)

Using US 5 (3.75mm) DPNs and **B**, CO 10 sts, PM, join to knit in the round.

Rounds 1–5: Knit.

Round 6: [K1, k2tog, k2] twice. (8 sts)

Round 7: Knit.

Round 8: [K2tog] 4 times. (4 sts)

Break yarn. Pull tail through remaining sts.

ASSEMBLY

Cut out all felt pieces using templates.

Use images as guides for positioning.

Glue eyes to face.

Glue inner ear to ears

Glue paw pads to feet

Sew head to body.

Sew belly to body.

Sew legs to body.

Curl ears slightly in and pin to head. Sew ears into place.

Sew curls to top of head in a row.

Use **D** and sewing needle to create a swirl at each side of hair curls.

Sew fringe to front edge of curls, with the long piece in the center.

Beginning in the center of the top of the rump, pin two tail sections. Sew into place. Sew additional tail sections along each side. Use a long length of **D** and a yarn needle to thread through each section, pulling them together to secure into place. Repeat as needed until secure.

Be sure to weave in all ends to ensure a smooth finish.

HAIR CURLS

LONG HAIR FRINGE

SHORT HAIR FRINGE

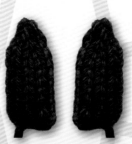

LAPRAS

OFFICIAL COLORS

NATIONAL POKÉDEX NO.	TYPE	WEIGHT	HEIGHT
0131	Water/ Ice	485.0 lbs/ 220.0 kg	8 ft 2 in/ 2.5 m

It ferries people across the sea on its back. It may sing an enchanting cry if it is in a good mood.

MATERIALS

- Cascade 220 (100% wool), 10-ply/ aran, 100g (220yd/200m), in the following shades:

- Robin Egg Blue(8905); 1 ball (**A**)

- Pear (8412); 1 ball (**B**)

- Iridescence (8872); 110yd/100m (**C**)

- Black (8555); Oddments (**D**)

- Set of five size US 5 (3.75mm) DPNs

- Felt pieces in black, white, and blue

- Fabric glue

- Polyester filling

GAUGE

22 sts and 26 rows measure 4 x 4in (10 x 10cm) over stockinette stitch (stocking stitch) using size US 5 (3.75mm) needles.

FINISHED SIZE

8½in (21cm) tall

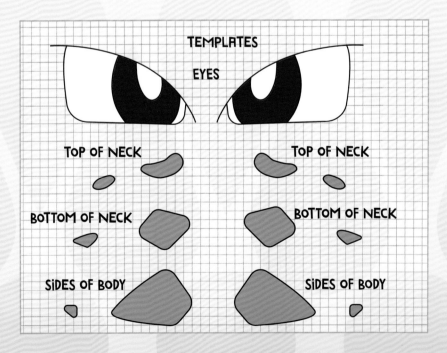

TEMPLATES

EYES

TOP OF NECK   TOP OF NECK

BOTTOM OF NECK   BOTTOM OF NECK

SIDES OF BODY   SIDES OF BODY

BODY (worked from the tail forward)

Using US 5 (3.75mm) DPNs and **A**, CO 4 sts, PM, join to knit in the round.

Round 1: [Kfb] 4 times. (8 sts)

Round 2: Knit.

Divide sts evenly between 4 DPNs, 2 sts on each needle.

Round 3: [K1, m1, k1] 4 times. (12 sts)

Round 4: Knit.

Round 5: [K2, m1, k2, m1, k2] twice. (16 sts)

Round 6: Knit.

Round 7: [K3, m1, k2, m1, k3] twice. (20 sts)

Round 8: Knit.

Round 9: K4, m1, k2, m1, k1, m1, k6, m1, k1, m1, k2, m1, k4. (26 sts)

Round 10: Knit.

Round 11:

Needle 1: Knit to last st on dpn, m1, k1.

Needle 2: K1, m1, knit to last 3 sts on dpn, m1, k3.

Needle 3: K3, m1, knit to last st on dpn, m1, k1.

Needle 4: K1, m1, knit to end of needle. (32 sts)

Repeat: Repeat rounds 10–11 eight more times until you have 74 sts.

Needle 1: 14 sts.

Needle 2: 23 sts.

Needle 3: 23 sts.

Needle 4: 14 sts.

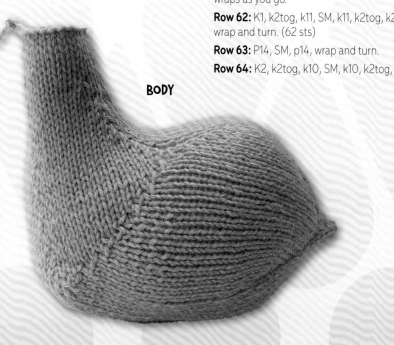

BODY

Rounds 26–35: Knit.

Round 36:

Needle 1: Knit.

Needle 2: Knit to last 5 sts on needle, k2tog, k3.

Needle 3: K3, k2tog. knit to end of needle.

Needle 4: Knit. (72 sts)

Round 37: Knit.

Repeat rounds 36–37 four more times until 64 sts remain.

Stuff body.

Begin shaping for neck:

Row 46: K28, wrap and turn.

Row 47: P28, SM, p28, wrap and turn.

Row 48: K28, SM, k26, wrap and turn.

Row 49: P26, SM, p26, wrap and turn.

Row 50: K26, SM, k24, wrap and turn.

Row 51: P24, SM, p24, wrap and turn.

Row 52: K24, SM, k22, wrap and turn.

Row 53: P22, SM, p22, wrap and turn.

Row 54: K22, SM, k20, wrap and turn.

Row 55: P20, SM, p20, wrap and turn.

Row 56: K20, SM, k18, wrap and turn.

Row 57: P18, SM, p18, wrap and turn.

Row 58: K18, SM, k16, wrap and turn.

Row 59: P16, SM, p16, wrap and turn.

Row 60: K16, SM, k14, wrap and turn.

Row 61: P14, SM, p14, wrap and turn.

Begin second turn, picking up and knitting wraps as you go.

Row 62: K1, k2tog, k11, SM, k11, k2tog, k2, wrap and turn. (62 sts)

Row 63: P14, SM, p14, wrap and turn.

Row 64: K2, k2tog, k10, SM, k10, k2tog, k4, wrap and turn. (60 sts)

Row 65: P15, SM, p15, wrap and turn.

Row 66: K4, k2tog, k9, SM, k9, k2tog, k6, wrap and turn. (58 sts)

Row 67: P16, SM, p16, wrap and turn.

Row 68: K16, SM, k18, wrap and turn.

Row 69: P18, SM, p18, wrap and turn.

Row 70: K8, k2tog, k8, SM, k8, k2tog, k10, wrap and turn. (56 sts)

Row 71: P19, SM, p19, wrap and turn.

Row 72: K19, SM, k21, wrap and turn.

Row 73: P21, SM, p21, wrap and turn.

Row 74: K12, k2tog, k7, SM, k7, k2tog, k14, wrap and turn. (54 sts)

Row 75: P22, SM, p22, wrap and turn, k22.

Round 76: Knit.

Round 77: K6, k2tog, k14, k2tog, k6, k2tog, k14, k2tog, k6. (50 sts)

Round 78: Knit.

Round 79: K20, k2tog, k6, k2tog, k20. (48 sts)

Round 80: Knit.

Round 81: K5, k2tog, k12, k2tog, k6, k2tog, k12, k2tog, k5. (44 sts)

Round 82: Knit.

Round 83: K17, k2tog, k6, k2tog, k17. (42 sts)

Round 84: Knit.

Round 85: K4, k2tog, k10, k2tog, k6, k2tog, k10, k2tog, k4. (38 sts)

Round 86: Knit.

Round 87: K14, k2tog, k6, k2tog, k14. (36 sts)

Round 88: Knit.

Round 89: K3, k2tog, k8, k2tog, k6, k2tog, k8, k2tog, k3. (32 sts)

Round 90: Knit.

Round 91: K11, k2tog, k6, k2tog, k11. (30 sts)

Round 92: Knit.

Round 93: K2, k2tog, k6, k2tog, k6, k2tog, k6, k2tog, k2. (26 sts)

Round 94: Knit.

Round 95: K8, k2tog, k6, k2tog, k8. (24 sts)

Rounds 96–100: Knit.

BO. Stuff neck.

PROJECT 17 / LAPRAS

HEAD

Using US 5 (3.75mm) DPNs and **A**, CO 4 sts, PM, join to knit in the round.

Round 1: [Kfb] 4 times. (8 sts)

Round 2: [Kfb] 8 times. (16 sts)

Round 3: Knit.

Round 4: [K1, m1, k2, m1, k1] 4 times. (24 sts)

Round 5: Knit.

Round 6: [K2, m1, k2, m1, k2] 4 times. (32 sts)

Round 7: Knit

Round 8: [K3, m1, k2, m1, k3] 4 times. (40 sts)

Round 9: Knit.

Round 10: [K3, m1, k4, m1, k3] 4 times. (48 sts)

Rounds 11–16: Knit.

Round 17: K9, k2tog, k6, k2tog, k6, k2tog, k14, k2tog, k5. (44 sts)

Rounds 18–19: Knit.

Round 20: K8, k2tog, k6, k2tog, k5, k2tog, k13, k2tog, k4. (40 sts)

Rounds 21–22: Knit.

Round 23: K7, k2tog, k5, k2tog, k5, k2tog, k11, k2tog, k4. (36 sts)

Rounds 24–25: Knit.

Round 26: K6, k2tog, k5, k2tog, k4, k2tog, k10, k2tog, k3. (32 sts)

Rounds 27–28: Knit.

Round 29: K5, k2tog, k4, k2tog, k4, k2tog, k8, k2tog, k3. (28 sts)

Round 30: Knit.

Round 31: K4, k2tog, k4, k2tog, k3, k2tog, k7, k2tog, k2. (24 sts)

Round 32: K3, k2tog, k3, k2tog, k3, k2tog, k5, k2tog, k2. (20 sts)

Stuff head.

Round 33: K2, k2tog, k3, k2tog, k2, k2tog, k4, k2tog, k1. (16 sts)

Round 34: K2tog, 8 times. (8 sts)

Round 35: K2tog, 4 times. (4 sts)

Break yarn, Pull tail through remaining sts. Weave in loose ends.

BELLY

Worked top down. Using US 5 (3.75mm) DPNs and **B**, CO 8 sts.

Rows 1–18: Complete in stockinette st, beginning with a knit row.

Row 19: K1, m1, knit to last st, m1, k1. (10 sts)

Rows 20–22: Complete in stockinette st.

Repeat: Repeat rows 19–22 four more times until you have 18 sts.

Row 39: K1, m1, knit to last st, m1, k1. (20 sts)

Rows 40: Purl.

Repeat rows 39–40 twice more until you have 24 sts

Rows 45–68: Complete in stockinette st.

Rows 69: K1, k2tog, knit to last 3 sts, k2tog, k1. (22 sts)

Row 70: Purl.

Repeat rows 69–70 until 6 sts remain.

Next row: K1, k2tog twice. K1. (4 sts)

Next row: Purl.

Next row: K2tog twice. (2 sts).

Break yarn, Pull tail through remaining sts. Weave in loose ends. Press lightly. Seam to underside of body.

CHiN

Using US 5 (3.75mm) DPNs and **B**, CO 12 sts.

Row 1: Kfb, k9, kfb, k1. (14 sts).

Row 2: Purl

Row 3: Knit.

Row 4: Purl.

Row 5: K1, k2tog, k8, k2tog, k1. (12 sts)

Row 6: BO 2 sts, (1 st left on right needle after cast off) p9. (10 sts)

Row 7: BO 2 sts, (1 st left on right needle after cast off) k7. (8 sts).

Row 8: Purl.

Row 9: Knit.

Row 10: P1, p2tog, p2, p2tog, p1. (6 sts)

Row 11: K2tog, k2, k2tog. (4 sts).

Row 12: [P2tog] twice. (2 sts)

Break yarn, Pull tail through remaining sts. Weave in loose ends. Press lightly.

HEAD

BELLY

SMALL FIN 1 (make one for upper left in A and one for lower right in B)

Using MC, CO 6 sts.

Row 1: Purl.

Row 2: K1, m1, knit to last st, m1, k1. (8 sts)

Row 3: Purl.

Row 4: K1, m1, knit to last st, m1, k1. (10 sts).

Row 5-9: Complete in stockinette st.

Row 10: K1, k2tog, Knit to end. (9 sts)

Row 11: Purl.

Row 12: K1, k2tog, knit to last 3 sts, k2tog, k1. (7 sts)

Row 13: Purl to last 3 sts, p2tog, p1. (6 sts)

Row 14: K1, k2tog, knit to last st, m1, k1.

Row 15: Purl to last 3 sts, p2tog, p1. (5 sts) BO row.

SMALL FIN 2 (make one for lower left in B and one for upper right in A)

Using MC, CO 6 sts.

Row 1: Purl.

Row 2: K1, m1, knit to last st, m1, k1. (8 sts)

Row 3: Purl.

Row 4: K1, m1, knit to last st, m1, k1. (10 sts).

Rows 5-9: Complete in stockinette st.

Row 10: K7, k2tog, k1. (9 sts)

Row 11: Purl.

Row 12: K1, k2tog, knit to last 3 sts, k2tog, k1. (7 sts)

Row 13: P4, p2tog, p1. (6 sts)

Row 14: K1, m1,k2, k2tog, k1.

Row 15: P1, p2tog, p3. (5 sts) BO.

LARGE FIN 1 (make one for upper left in A, and one for lower right in B)

Using US 5 (3.75mm) DPNs CO 9 sts.

Row 1: Purl.

Row 2: Knit to last st, m1, k1. (10 sts)

Repeat rows 1 and 2 six more times. (16 sts)

Row 15: Purl.

Row 16: K1. k2tog, knit to last st, m1, k1.

Repeat rows 15 and 16 five more times.

Row 27: P1, m1, purl to last st, p2tog, p1.

Row 28: K1. k2tog, knit to last st, m1, k1. BO purlwise.

LARGE FIN 2 (knit one for lower left in A and one for lower right in B)

Using US 5 (3.75mm) DPNs CO 9 sts.

Row 1: Purl.

Row 2: K1, m1, knit to end. (10 sts)

Repeat rows 1–2 six more times. (16 sts)

Row 15: Purl.

Row 16: K1. m1, knit to last st, k2tog, k1.

Repeat rows 15–16 five more times.

Row 27: P1, p2tog, purl to last st, m1, p1.

Row 28: K1. m1, knit to last st, k2tog, k1.

Repeat: Repeat rows 23–24 once more. BO purlwise.

CHIN

SMALL FINS 1

SMALL FINS 2

LARGE FINS 1

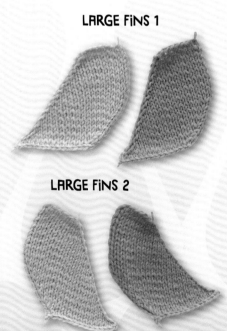

LARGE FINS 2

SADDLE

Using US 5 (3.75mm) DPNs and **C**, CO 28 sts.

Rows 1 (RS): Knit.
Row 2: Purl.
Row 3: K1, k2tog, k22, k2tog, k1. (26 sts)
Row 4: Purl.
Row 5: K1, k2tog, k20, k2tog, k1. (24 sts)
Row 6: Purl.
Row 7: K1, k2tog, k18, k2tog, k1. (22 sts)
Row 8: Purl.
Row 9: K1, k2tog, k16, k2tog, k1. (20 sts)
Rows 10–14: Work in stockinette st.
Row 15: K1, m1, k18, m1, k1. (22 sts)
Row 16: Purl.
Row 17: K1, m1, k20, m1, k1. (24 sts)
Row 18: Purl.
Row 19: K1, m1, k22, m1, k1. (26 sts)
Row 20: Purl.
Row 21: K1, m1, k24, m1, k1. (28 sts)
Row 22: Purl.
Row 23: Knit.
Row 24: Purl.
Row 25: K9, k2tog, k6, k2tog, k9. (26 sts)
Row 26: P8, p2tog, p6, p2tog, p8. (24 sts)
Row 27: K7, k2tog, k6, k2tog, k7. (22 sts)
Row 28: P6, p2tog, p6, p2tog, p6. (20 sts)
Row 29: K5, k2tog, k6, k2tog, k5. (18 sts)
Row 30: P4, p2tog, p6, p2tog, p4. (16 sts)

Row 31: K3, k2tog, k6, k2tog, k3. (14 sts)
Row 32: P2, p2tog, p6, p2tog, p2. (12 sts)
Row 33: K1, k2tog, k6, k2tog, k1. (10 sts)
Row 34: P2tog, p6, p2tog. (8 sts)
Row 35: K2tog, k4, k2tog. (6 sts)
Border: Leaving 6 working sts on DPN, use working yarn and DPNs, and with right side facing, continue to pick up a border around the edge of saddle as follows:

Pick up and knit 8 sts down left diagonal side of saddle.

Round 36: Pick up and knit 8 sts along right diagonal side of saddle.

15 sts along right side of saddle,.

28 sts along cast-on edge of saddle.

15 sts along left side of saddle.

8 sts along left diagonal side of saddle.

Knit across 6 working sts, PM, join to knit in the round. (80 sts)

Round 37: Purl one row.

BO knitwise.

SADDLE LUMPS (make 8)

Using US 5 (3.75mm) and **C**, CO 3 sts, PM, join to knit in the round.

Round 1: [Kfb] 3 times. (6 sts)
Round 2: [Kfb, k1] 3 times. (9 sts)

Knit 5 rounds. BO. Stuff. Weave in loose ends.

Rounds 3–7: Knit.

BO. Stuff. Weave in loose ends.

EARS (make 2)

Using US 5 (3.75mm) DPNs and **A**, CO 10 sts, PM, join to knit in the round.

Round 1: [Kfb, k2, kfb, k1] twice. (14 sts)
Round 2: Knit.
Round 3: [K1, m1, k5, m1, k1] twice. (18 sts)
Rounds 4–6: Knit.
Round 7: [K1, k2tog, k3, k2tog, k1] twice. (14 sts)
Round 8: Knit.
Round 9: [K1, k2tog, k1, k2tog, k1] twice. (10 sts)
Round 10: Knit.
Round 11: [K2tog] 5 times. (5 sts)

Break yarn, Pull tail through remaining sts. Stuff ears.

HORN

Using US 5 (3.75mm) DPNs and **A**, CO 10 sts, PM, join to knit in the round.

Round 1: Knit.
Round 2: [K1, K2tog, k2] twice. (8 sts)
Round 3: Knit.
Round 4: [K1, k2tog, k1] twice. (6 sts)
Round 5: Knit.
Round 6: [K2tog, k1] twice. (4 sts)

Break yarn, Pull tail through remaining sts.

EARS

SADDLE

SADDLE LUMPS

ASSEMBLY

Cut out all felt pieces using templates.

Use images as guides for positioning.

Glue felt pieces for eyes.

Glue felt pieces for spots.

Sew head to body.

Sew stripe to body and tail.

Sew chin to bottom of head.

Sew top and bottom of fins together and stuff.

Sew fins to body.

Sew ears to head.

Pin saddle onto back and sew into place.

Sew lumps to saddle as shown.

Use yarn **D** to embroider nostrils, eyebrows, and upper eye border.

Use yarn **D** to embroider swirls in ears.

Be sure to weave in all ends to ensure a smooth finish.

HORN

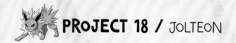

JOLTEON

OFFICIAL COLORS

NATIONAL POKÉDEX NO.	TYPE	WEIGHT	HEIGHT
0135	Electric	54.0 lbs/ 24.5 kg	2 ft 7 in/ 0.8 m

It concentrates the weak electric charges emitted by its cells and launches wicked lightning bolts.

MATERIALS

- Cascade 220 (100% wool), 10-ply/ aran, 100g (220yd/200m), in the following shades:

- Neon Yellow (7828); 2 balls (**A**)

- White (8505); 1 ball (**B**)

- Black (8555); Oddments (**C**)

- Pieces of felt in black, white, and pink

- Fabric glue

- Polyester filling

GAUGE

22 sts and 26 rows measure 4 x 4in (10 x 10cm) over stockinette stitch (stocking stitch) using US 5 (3.75mm) needles.

FINISHED SIZE

11in (28cm) long

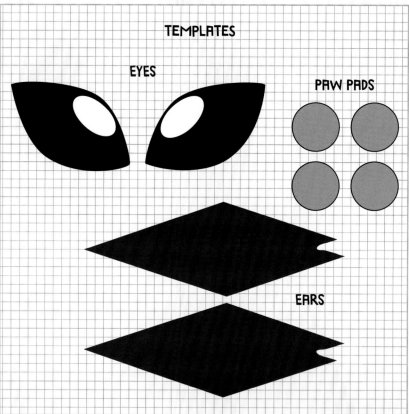

TEMPLATES

EYES

PAW PADS

EARS

HEAD

Using US 5 (3.75mm) DPNs, and **A**, CO 4 sts, PM, join to knit in the round.

Round 1: [Kfb] 4 times. (8 sts)

Round 2: [Kfb] 8 times. (16 sts)

Round 3: Knit.

Round 4: [K1, m1, k2, m1, k1] 4 times. (24 sts)

Rounds 5–6: Knit.

Round 7: K5, m1, k3, m1, k2, m1, k3, m1, k7, m1, k2, m1, k2. (30 sts)

Round 8: Knit.

Round 9: K6, m1, k10, m1, knit to end. (32 sts)

Round 10: Knit.

Round 11: K7, m1, k3, m1, k4, m1, k3, m1, k9, m1, k4, m1, k2. (38 sts)

Round 12: Knit.

Round 13: K8, m1, k12, m1, knit to end. (40 sts)

Round 14: Knit.

Round 15: K9, m1, k3, m1, k6, m1, k3, m1, k11, m1, k6, m1, k2. (46 sts)

Round 16: Knit.

Round 17: K10, m1, k14, m1, knit to end. (48 sts)

Round 18: Knit.

Round 19: K11, m1, k3, m1, k8, m1, k3, m1, k13, m1, k8, m1, k2. (54 sts)

Round 20: Knit.

Round 21: K12, m1, k16, m1, knit to end. (56 sts)

Rounds 22–23: Knit.

Row 24: K41, wrap and turn.

Row 25: P40, wrap and turn.

Row 26: K36, wrap and turn.

Row 27: P32, wrap and turn.

Row 28: K28, wrap and turn.

Row 29: P24, wrap and turn.

Row 30: K26, wrap and turn.

Row 31: P28, wrap and turn.

Row 32: K32, wrap and turn.

Row 33: P36, wrap and turn, knit to marker.

Round 34: Knit.

Round 35: [K2, k2tog, k6, k2tog, k2] 4 times. (48 sts)

Round 36: Knit.

Round 37: [K2, k2tog, k4, k2tog, k2] 4 times. (40 sts)

Round 38: Knit.

BO. Stuff head.

BODY

Using US 5 (3.75mm) DPNs, and **A**, CO 4 sts, PM, join to knit in the round.

Round 1: [Kfb] 4 times. (8 sts)

Round 2: Knit.

Round 3: [Kfb] 8 times. (16 sts)

Divide sts evenly between 4 DPNs, 4 sts per needle.

Round 4: Knit.

Round 5: [K1, m1, k2, m1, k1] 4 times. (24 sts)

Round 6: Knit.

Round 7: [K2, m1, knit to last 2 sts on needle, m1, k2] 4 times (32 sts)

Repeat rounds 6–7 until you have 56 sts, 14 per needle.

Continue in stockinette st until piece measures 4¼in (10.8cms).

Place markers for rump spikes:

Next round: K4, place removable stitch marker on the last worked st. K35, place removable stitch marker on the last worked st knit, k17.

Work straight until piece measures 6½in (16.5cm).

Next round: [K2, k2tog, knit to last 4 sts on needle, k2tog, k2] 4 times. (48 sts)

Next round: Knit.

Repeat last two rounds until you have 24 sts, 6 sts per needle.

Stuff body.

Next round: [K1, k2tog twice, k1] 4 times. (16 sts)

Next round: [K2tog] 8 times. (8 sts)

Next round: [K2tog] 4 times. (4 sts)

Break yarn, pull tail through remaining sts. Weave in loose ends.

REAR SPiKES

Using US 5 (3.75mm) DPNs, pick up 34 sts in a straight line between stitch markers

REAR SPiKES

HEAD

BODY

on top of body. Join **A**, and begin knitting towards the BO end of the body.

Row 1 (RS): Knit.

Row 2: Purl.

Row 3: K1, m1, k8, m1, k4, m1, k8, m1, k4, m1, k8, m1, k1. (40 sts)

Row 4: Purl.

Row 5: Knit.

Row 6: Purl.

Row 7: K1, m1, k9, m1, k6, m1, k8, m1, k6, m1, k9, m1, k1. (46 sts)

Row 8: Purl.

Row 9: Knit.

Row 10: Purl.

Row 11: K1, m1, k10, m1, k8, m1, k8, m1, k8, m1, k10, m1, k1. (52 sts)

Break yarn.

Cut 8, 6–8in (15–20cm) lengths of scrap yarn. Divide knit sts onto pieces of scrap yarn as follows for spikes:

Spike 1: Slip 7 sts onto scrap yarn.

Spike 2: Slip 6 sts onto scrap yarn.

Spike 3: Slip 6 sts onto scrap yarn.

Spike 4: Slip 7 sts onto scrap yarn.

Spike 5: Slip 7 sts onto scrap yarn.

Spike 6: Slip 6 sts onto scrap yarn.

Spike 7: Slip 6 sts onto scrap yarn.

Spike 8: Slip 7 sts onto scrap yarn.

Using 1 DPN and **A**, CO 40 sts for underside of spikes. Move these 40 sts onto a long piece of scrap yarn.

Spike 1: Starting with the sts above the left hind leg, place the first 7 sts for Spike 1 onto a DPN. Place first 5 sts from long length of scrap yarn on another DPN.

Round 1: Using **A**, k7 across 1st needle, CO 2, k5 from 2nd needle, PM, join to knit in the round. (14 sts)

Round 2: Knit.

Round 3: [K3, k2tog, k2] twice. (12 sts)

Round 4: Knit.

Round 5: [K2, k2tog, k2] twice. (10 sts)

Round 6: Knit.

Round 7: [K2, k2tog, k1] twice. (8 sts)

Round 8: Knit.

Round 9: [K2tog] 4 times. (4 sts)

Round 10: [K2tog] twice (2 sts)

Break yarn, pull tail through remaining sts. Weave in loose ends.

Spike 2: Place next 6 sts for Spike 2 onto a DPN. Place the next 5 sts from the length of scrap yarn onto a 2nd DPN.

Round 1: Beginning with the 6 sts and using **A**, k6, CO 3, k5 from 2nd DPN, pick up and k2 from inner edge of spike 1, PM, join to knit in the round. (16 sts)

Rounds 2–3: Knit.

Round 4: [K3, k2tog, k3] twice. (14 sts)

Rounds 5–7: Knit.

Round 8: [K2, k2tog, k3] twice. (12 sts)

Rounds 9–11: Knit.

Round 12: [K2, k2tog, k2] twice. (10 sts)

Rounds 13–15: Knit.

Round 16: [K2, k2tog, k1] twice. (8 sts)

Rounds 17–18: Knit.

Round 19: [K2tog] 4 times. (4 sts)

Break yarn, pull tail through remaining sts. Weave in loose ends.

Spike 3: Place next 6 sts for Spike 3 onto a DPN. Place the next 5 sts from the length of scrap yarn onto a 2nd DPN.

Round 1: Beginning with the 6 sts and **A**, k6, CO 4 sts, k5 from 2nd DPN, pick up and k3 from inner edge of spike 2, PM, join to knit in the round. (18 sts)

Rounds 2–3: Knit.

Round 4: [K3, k2tog, k4] twice. (16 sts)

Rounds 5–7: Knit.

Round 8: [K3, k2tog, k3] twice. (14 sts)

Rounds 9–11: Knit.

Round 12: [K2, k2tog, k3] twice. (12 sts)

Rounds 13–14: Knit.

Round 15: [K2, k2tog, k2] twice. (10 sts)

Rounds 16–17: Knit.

Round 18: [K2, k2tog, k1] twice. (8 sts)

Rounds 19–20: Knit.

Round 21: [K2tog] 4 times. (4 sts)

Break yarn, pull tail through remaining sts. Weave in loose ends.

Spike 4: Place next 7 sts for Spike 4 onto a DPN. Place the next 5 sts from the length of scrap yarn onto a 2nd DPN.

Round 1: Beginning with the 7 sts and **A**, k7, CO 5 sts, k5 from 2nd DPN, pick up and k4

from inner edge of spike 3, pm, join to knit in the round. (21 sts)

Rounds 2–3: Knit.

Round 4: [K5, k2tog] 3 times. (18 sts)

Rounds 5–7: Knit.

Round 8: [K3, k2tog, k4] twice. (16 sts)

Rounds 9–10: Knit.

Round 11: [K3, k2tog, k3] twice. (14 sts)

Rounds 12–13: Knit.

Round 14: [K2, k2tog, k3] twice. (12 sts)

Rounds 15–16: Knit.

Round 17: [K2, k2tog, k2] twice. (10 sts)

Rounds 18–19: Knit.

Round 20: [K2, k2tog, k1] twice. (8 sts)

Rounds 21–22: Knit.

Round 23: [K2tog] 4 times. (4 sts)

Break yarn, pull tail through remaining sts. Weave in loose ends.

Spike 5: Place next 7 sts for Spike 5 onto a DPN. Place the next 5 sts from the length of scrap yarn onto a 2nd DPN.

Round 1: Beginning with the 7 sts, k7, CO 4 sts, k5 from 2nd DPN, pick up and k5 from inner edge of spike 4, PM, join to knit in the round. (21 sts)

Rounds 2–23: Repeat from Spike 4.

Spike 6: Place next 6 sts for Spike 6 onto a DPN. Place the next 5 sts from the length of scrap yarn onto a 2nd DPN.

Round 1: Beginning with the 6 sts and **A**, k6, CO3, k5 from 2nd DPN, pick up and k4 from inner edge of spike 5, pm, join to knit in the round. 18 sts

Rounds 2–21: Repeat from Spike 3.

Spike 7: Place next 6 sts for Spike 7 onto a DPN. Place the next 5 sts from the length of scrap yarn onto a 2nd DPN.

Round 1: Beginning with the 6 sts and **A**, k6, CO2, k5 from 2nd DPN, pick up and k3 from inner edge of spike 6. (16 sts)

Rounds 2–19: Repeat from Spike 2.

Spike 8: Place the remaining 7 sts for Spike 8 onto a DPN. Place remaining 5 sts from long length of scrap yarn on another DPN.

Round 1: Using **A**, k7 across 1st DPN, k5 from 2nd DPN, CO 2 sts from inner edge of spike 7, pm, join to knit in the round. (14 sts)

Rounds 2–10: Repeat from Spike 1.

Stuff all spikes. You will seam them into place after completing the other pieces.

HiND LEGS (make 2)

Using US 5 (3.75mm) DPNs and **A**, CO 4 sts, PM, join to knit in the round.

Round 1: [Kfb] 4 times. (8 sts)

Round 2: [Kfb] 8 times. (16 sts)

Round 3: [K2, m1, k2] 4 times. (20 sts)

Round 4: [K1, m1, k3, m1, k6] twice. (24 sts)

Rounds 5–8: Knit.

Round 9: K5, k2tog, k5, k2tog, knit to end. (22 sts)

Round 10: K4, k2tog, k5, k2tog, knit to end. (20 sts)

Round 11: K3, k2tog, k5, k2tog, knit to end. (18 sts)

Rounds 12–21: Knit.

Row 22: K3, wrap and turn.

Row 24: P3, sm, p8, wrap and turn.

Row 25: K8, sm, k2, wrap and turn.

Row 26: P2, sm, p7, wrap and turn.

Row 27: K7, sm, k1, wrap and turn.

Row 28: P1, sm, p6, wrap and turn.

Row 29: K6, sm, k2, wrap and turn.

Row 30: P2, sm, p7, wrap and turn.

Row 31: K7, sm, k3, wrap and turn.

Row 32: P3, sm, p8, wrap and turn, knit to marker.

Round 33: Knit.

Round 34: K1, m1, k11, m1, k6. (20 sts)

Round 35: Knit.

Round 36: K1, m1, k13, m1, k6. (22 sts)

Round 37: Knit.

Round 38: K1, m1, k15, m1, k6. (24 sts)

Round 39: Knit.

Round 40: K1, m1, k17, m1, k6. (26 sts)

Begin top of leg.

Left leg

Round 41: K21, BO5. (21 sts)

Continue working in rows.

Round 42: K1, m1, knit to last 2 sts, k2tog.

Row 43: P2tog, purl to end. (20 sts)

Row 44: Knit to last 2 sts, k2tog. (19 sts)

Rows 45–48: Repeat rows 43–44 until 15 sts remain.

Row 49: BO 6 sts, purl to end. (9 sts)

Row 50: K1, k2tog, k3, k2tog, k1. (7 sts) BO.

Right leg

Round 41: K21, BO 5 sts. (21 sts)

Continue working in rows.

Row 42: K2tog, k18, m1, k1.

Row 43: Purl to last 2 sts, p2tog. (20 sts)

Row 44: K2tog, knit to last 2 sts. (19 sts)

Row 45: Purl to last 2 sts, p2tog. (18 sts)

Rows 46–47: Repeat rounds 44–45 until 16 sts remain.

Row 48: BO 7 sts, knit to end. (9 sts)

Row 49: Purl.

Row 50: K1, k2tog, k3, k2tog, k1. (7 sts) BO.

FRONT LEGS (make 2)

Using US 5 (3.75mm) DPNs and **A**, CO 4 sts, PM, join to knit in the round.

Round 1: [Kfb] 4 times. (8 sts)

Round 2: [Kfb] 8 times. (16 sts)

Round 3: [K2, m1, k2] 4 times. (20 sts)

Round 4: [K1, m1, k3, m1, k6] twice. (24 sts)

Rounds 5–8: Knit.

Round 9: K5, k2tog, k5, k2tog, knit to end. (22 sts)

Round 10: K4, k2tog, k5, k2tog, knit to end. (20 sts)

Rounds 11–23: Knit.

Round 24: K1, m1, k13, m1, k6. (22 sts)

Round 25: Knit.

Round 26: K1, m1, k2, k2tog, k7, k2tog, k2, m1, k6.

Round 27: Knit.

Round 28: K1, m1, k15, m1, k6. (24 sts)

Round 29: Knit.

Round 30: K1, m1, k3, k2tog, k7, k2tog, k3, m1, k6.

Round 31: Knit.

Round 28: K1, m1, k22, m1, k6. (26 sts)

Round 29: Knit.

Round 30: K1, m1, k4, k2tog, k7, k2tog, k4, m1, k6.

Round 31: Knit.

Begin top of leg.

Right leg:

Row 32: BO 8 sts, (1 st left on right needle after cast off) k15, k2tog. (17 sts)

Continue working in rows.

HiND LEGS

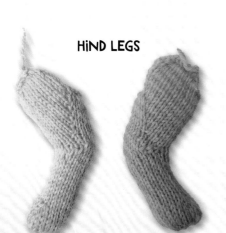

FRONT LEGS

Row 33: Purl to last 2 sts, p2tog. (16 sts)

Row 34: Knit to last 2 sts, k2tog. (15 sts)

Rows 35–38: Repeat rows 33–34 until 11 sts remain.

Row 39: P1, p2tog, p5, p2tog, p1. (9 sts)

Row 40: K1, k2tog, k3, k2tog, k1. (7 sts) BO. Stuff leg.

Left leg

Row 32: K13, BO 8 sts, k2tog, k3. (17 sts)

Continue working in rows, without turning for the next row.

Row 33: Knit to last 2 sts, k2tog. (16 sts)

Row 34: Purl to last 2 sts, p2tog. (15 sts)

Repeat rows 33–34 until 11 sts remain.

Row 39: K1, k2tog, k5, k2tog, k1. (9 sts)

Row 40: P1, p2tog, p3, p2tog, p1. (7 sts) BO. Stuff leg.

REAR TAIL SPIKES (make 3)

Using US 5 (3.75mm) DPNs and **A**, CO 20 sts, PM, join to knit in the round.

Round 1: Knit.

Round 2: [K4, k2tog, k4] twice. (18 sts)

Round 3: Knit.

Round 4: [K4, k2tog, k3] twice. (16 sts)

Round 5: Knit.

Round 6: [K3, k2tog, k3] twice. (14 sts)

Round 7: Knit.

Round 8: [K3, k2tog, k2] twice. (12 sts)

Round 9: Knit.

Round 10: [K2, k2tog, k2] twice. (10 sts)

Round 11: Knit.

Round 12: [K2, k2tog, k1] twice. (8 sts)

Round 13: Knit.

Round 14: [K1, k2tog, k1] twice. (6 sts)

Round 15: Knit.

Round 16: [K1, k2tog] twice. (4 sts)

Break yarn, pull tail through remaining sts. Weave in loose ends. Stuff all tail spikes.

LARGE COLLAR BASE (make 2):

Using US 5 (3.75mm) DPNs and **B**, CO 32 sts, PM, join to knit in the round. Divide sts evenly between 4 DPNs, 8 per DPN.

Round 1: Knit.

Round 2: [K3, m1, knit to last 3 sts on DPN, m1, k3] 4 times. (40 sts)

Repeat: Repeat rounds 1–2 until you have 80 sts, 20 on each DPN.

Knit one round. Move sts to scrap yarn.

Repeat for 2nd collar base. Leave working yarn attached.

LARGE COLLAR SPIKES

Place both sides of collar with purl sides together. Line up increase seams and last st.

Collar spike 1

Place first 5 sts from scrap yarn on a DPN. Place 5 corresponding sts from other side of collar on a DPN. [see figure 1 below]. (10 sts)

Rounds 1–5: Knit.

Round 6: [K1, k2tog, k2] twice. (8 sts)

Rounds 7–10: Knit.

Round 11: [K1, k2tog, k1] twice. (6 sts)

Rounds 12–15: Knit.

Round 16: [K2tog] 3 times. (3 sts)

Break yarn, pull tail through remaining sts. Weave in loose ends.

figure 1

REAR TAIL SPIKES (make 3)

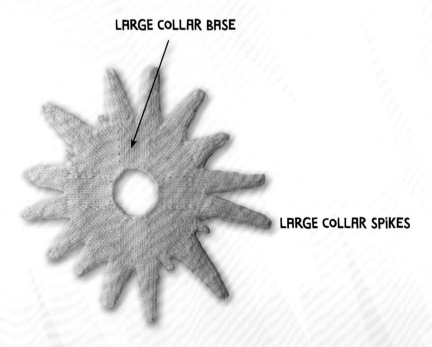

LARGE COLLAR BASE

LARGE COLLAR SPIKES

Collar spike 2

Place next 2 sts from scrap yarn on a DPN. Place 2 corresponding sts from other side of collar on a DPN. (4 sts)

Rounds 1–3: Knit.

Round 4: [K2tog] twice. (2 sts)

Break yarn, pull tail through remaining sts. Weave in loose ends.

Collar spike 3

Place next 6 sts from scrap yarn on a DPN. Place 6 corresponding sts from other side of collar on a DPN. (12 sts)

Rounds 1–4: Knit.

Round 5: [K2, k2tog, k2] twice. (10 sts)

Rounds 6–9: Knit.

Round 10: [K1, k2tog, k2] twice. (8 sts)

Rounds 11–14: Knit.

Round 15: [K1, k2tog, k1] twice. (6 sts)

Rounds 16–18: Knit.

Round 19: [K2tog] 3 times. (3 sts)

Break yarn, pull tail through remaining sts. Weave in loose ends.

Collar spike 4

Repeat instructions for Spike 2.

Collar spikes 5 and 6

Repeat instructions for Spike 1.

Collar spike 7

Place first 5 sts from scrap yarn on a DPN. Place 5 corresponding sts from other side of collar on a DPN. (10 sts)

Rounds 1–4: Knit.

Round 5: [K1, k2tog, k2] twice. (8 sts)

Rounds 6–9: Knit.

Round 10: [K1, k2tog, k1] twice. (6 sts)

Rounds 11–13: Knit.

Round 14: [K2tog] 3 times. (3 sts)

Break yarn, pull tail through remaining sts. Weave in loose ends.

Collar spike 8

Place first 5 sts from scrap yarn on a DPN. Place 5 corresponding sts from other side of collar on a DPN. (10 sts)

Rounds 1–2: Knit.

Round 3: [K1, k2tog, k2] twice. (8 sts)

Rounds 4–6: Knit.

Round 7: [K1, k2tog, k1] twice. (6 sts)

Rounds 8–10: Knit.

Round 11: [K2tog] 3 times. (3 sts)

Break yarn, pull tail through remaining sts. Weave in loose ends.

Collar spikes 9 and 10

Repeat instructions for Spike 1.

Collar spike 11

Repeat instructions for Spike 2.

Collar spike 12

Repeat instructions for Spike 3.

Collar spike 13

Repeat instructions for Spike 2.

Collar spikes 14 and 15

Repeat instructions for Spike 1.

Collar spike 16

Repeat instructions for Spike 8.

Collar spike 17

Repeat instructions for Spike 7.

Collar spike 18

Repeat instructions for Spike 1.

Weave in all lose ends. Seam together cast on edges. Press lightly.

SMALL SPIKE COLLAR

Using US 5 (3.75mm) DPNs and **A**, CO 5 sts.

Row 1: Knit.

Row 2: K3, k2tog. (4 sts)

Row 3: Knit.

Row 4: K2, k2tog. (3 sts)

Row 5: Knit.

Row 6: K1, k2tog. (2 sts)

Row 7: K2tog.

Row 8: K1, CO4. (5 sts)

Repeat: Repeat rows 1–8 five more times, then repeat rows 1–7 once more. Break yarn, pull tail through remaining st. Press lightly.

SMALL SPIKE COLLAR

EARS (make 2)

Using US 5 (3.75mm) DPNs and **A**, CO 12 sts, PM, join to knit in the round.

Rounds 1–3: Knit.

Round 4: [K1, m1, k4, m1, k1] twice. (16 sts)

Rounds 5–7: Knit.

Round 8: [K1, m1, k6, m1, k1] twice. (20 sts)

Rounds 9–11: Knit.

Round 12: [K1, m1, k8, m1, k1] twice. (24 sts)

Rounds 13–15: Knit.

Round 16: [K1, m1, k10, m1, k1] twice. (28 sts)

Round 17: Knit.

Round 18: [K1, k2tog, k8, k2tog, k1] twice. (24 sts)

Rounds 19–21: Knit.

Round 22: [K1, k2tog, k6, k2tog, k1] twice. (20 sts)

Rounds 23–25: Knit.

Round 26: [K1, k2tog, k4, k2tog, k1] twice. (16 sts)

Rounds 27–29: Knit.

Round 30: [K1, k2tog, k2, k2tog, k1] twice. (12 sts)

Rounds 31–33: Knit.

Round 34: [K1, k2tog twice, k1] twice. (8 sts)

Round 35: Knit.

Round 36: [K2tog] 4 times. (4 sts)

Break yarn, pull tail through remaining sts. Weave in loose ends.

ASSEMBLY

Cut out all felt pieces using templates.

Use images as guides for positioning.

Glue felt pieces for eyes, ears, and feet pads.

Sew small spike collar to upper curve of neck.

Sew large collar to body behind the small collar, at a slight angle as shown.

Sew head to body, centered over collar.

Sew legs to bottom of body.

Sew ears to head.

Sew three tail spikes to rear as in image.

Stretch edges of the back stripes firmly over hips and pin into place just below top line of hind legs. Sew sides and back edge into place, stuffing as you go.

Use **D** to embroider nostrils.

Be sure to weave in all ends to ensure a smooth finish.

EARS

FLAREON

OFFICIAL COLORS

NATIONAL POKÉDEX NO.	TYPE	WEIGHT	HEIGHT
0136	Fire	55.1 lbs/ 25.0 kg	2 ft 11 in/ 0.9 m

Inhaled air is carried to its flame sac, heated, and exhaled as fire that reaches over 3,000 degrees Fahrenheit (1,649 °C) .

MATERIALS

- Cascade 220 (100% wool), 10-ply/ aran, 100g (220yd/200m), in the following shades:

- Jack O'Lantern (7824); 1 ball (**A**)

- Butter (8687); 1 ball (**B**) (alternatively, may use pale yellow roving for collar and tail)

- Black (8555); Oddments (**C**)

- Set of five size US 5 (3.75mm) DPNs

- Felt pieces in black, white, and red

- Fabric glue

- Polyester filling

GAUGE

22 sts and 26 rows measure 4 x 4in (10 x 10cm) over stockinette stitch (stocking stitch) using size US 5 (3.75mm) needles

FINISHED SIZE

14in (35.5cm) tall

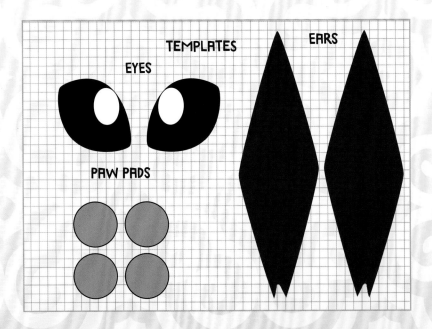

TEMPLATES

EYES

EARS

PAW PADS

HEAD AND BODY (worked from tail to head)

Using US 5 (3.75mm) DPNs and **A**, CO 4 sts, PM, join to knit in the round.

Round 1: [Kfb] 4 times. (8 sts)

Round 2: [Kfb] 8 times. (16 sts)

Round 3: Knit.

Round 4: [K1, m1, k2, m1, k1] 4 times. (24 sts)

Round 5: Knit.

Round 6: [K2, m1, k2, m1, k2] 4 times. (32 sts)

Round 7: Knit

Round 8: [K3, m1, k2, m1, k3] 4 times. (40 sts)

Round 9: Knit.

Round 10: [K3, m1, k4, m1, k3] 4 times. (48 sts)

Rounds 11–33: Knit.

Begin turn for chest.

Row 34: K35, wrap and turn.

Row 35: P34, wrap and turn.

Row 36: K33, wrap and turn.

Row 37: P32, wrap and turn.

Row 38: K31, wrap and turn.

Row 39: P30, wrap and turn.

Row 40: K29, wrap and turn.

Row 41: P28, wrap and turn.

Row 42: K27, wrap and turn.

Row 43: P26, wrap and turn.

Row 44: K25, wrap and turn.

Row 45: P24, wrap and turn.

Row 46: K23, wrap and turn.

Row 47: P22, wrap and turn.

Row 48: K21, wrap and turn.

Row 49: P20, wrap and turn.

Row 50: K19, wrap and turn.

Row 51: P18, wrap and turn.

Row 52: K17, wrap and turn.

Row 53: P16, wrap and turn.

Row 54: K15, wrap and turn.

Row 55: P14, wrap and turn, knit to end.

Rounds 56–57: Knit.

Round 58: K1, k2tog, k30, k2tog, knit to end. (46 sts)

Round 59: Knit.

Round 60: K1, k2tog, k28, k2tog, knit to end. (44 sts)

Rounds 61–62: Knit.

Round 63: [K12, k2tog, k4, k2tog, k2] twice. (40 sts)

Rounds 64–65: Knit.

Stuff body.

Begin turn for head, slip marker as you get to it.

Row 66: K9, wrap and turn.

Row 67: P28, wrap and turn.

Row 68: K11, m1, k6, m1, k9, wrap and turn. (42 sts)

Row 69: P26, wrap and turn.

Row 70: K24, wrap and turn.

Row 71: P22, wrap and turn.

Row 72: K20, wrap and turn.

Row 73: P18, wrap and turn.

Row 74: K16, wrap and turn.

Row 75: P14, wrap and turn.

Begin second turn. Pick up and knit wraps as you go.

Row 76: K15, wrap and turn.

Row 77: P16, wrap and turn.

Row 78: K18, wrap and turn.

Row 79: P20, wrap and turn.

Row 80: K22, wrap and turn.

Row 81: P24, wrap and turn.

Row 82: K26, wrap and turn.

Row 83: P28, wrap and turn, knit to end.

Rounds 84–88: Knit.

Round 89: K1, k2tog, k24, k2tog, knit to end. (40 sts)

Rounds 90–93: Knit.

Round 94: K1, k2tog, k22, k2tog, k3, k2tog, k4, k2tog, k2. (36 sts)

Round 95: Knit.

Round 96: [K10, k2tog, k2, k2tog, k2] twice. (32 sts)

Stuff head.

Round 97: Knit.

Round 98: K1, k2tog, k18, k2tog, knit to end. (30 sts)

Round 99: K1, k2tog, k5, k2tog, k2, k2tog, k5, k2tog, k2, k2tog, k2, k2tog, k1. (24 sts)

Round 100: K2tog, k14, k2tog, knit to end. (22 sts)

Round 101: K2tog, k4, [k2tog] twice, k4, k2tog, k1, [k2tog] twice, k1. (16 sts)

Round 102: K2tog, k8, k2tog, knit to end. (14 sts)

Round 103: K2tog, k1, [k2tog] twice, k1, [k2tog] 3 times. (8 sts)

Round 104: Knit.

Stuff head.

Round 105: [K2tog] 4 times. (4 sts)

Break yarn, pull tail through remaining sts, and pull loose end into inside of fabric.

HEAD AND BODY

PROJECT 19 / FLAREON

FRONT LEGS (make 2)

Using US 5 (3.75mm) DPNs and **A**, CO 4 sts, PM, join to knit in the round.

Round 1: [Kfb] 4 times. (8 sts)

Round 2: [Kfb] 8 times. (16 sts)

Round 3: [K2, m1, k2] 4 times. (20 sts)

Round 4: [K1, m1, k3, m1, k6] twice. (24 sts)

Rounds 5–8: Knit.

Round 9: K5, k2tog, k5, k2tog, knit to end. (22 sts)

Round 10: K4, k2tog, k5, k2tog, knit to end. (20 sts)

Rounds 11–18: Knit.

Begin upper portion of leg.

Right leg

Round 19: BO 5 sts (1 st left on right needle after BO), k12, k2tog, turn. (14 sts)

Continue knitting in rows.

Row 20: Purl to last 2 sts, p2tog. (13 sts)

Row 21: Knit to last 2 sts, k2tog. (12 sts)

Repeat rows 20 and 21 until 5 sts remain. BO.

Left leg

Round 19: K10, BO 5, slip last st on right needle back to left needle, k2tog, k3, remove marker. (14 sts)

Continue knitting in rows, working in the same direction as round 19 for the first row.

Row 20: Knit to last 2 sts before the BO sts on round 19, k2tog. (13 sts)

Row 21: Purl to last 2 sts, p2tog. (12 sts)

Repeat rows 20 and 21 until 5 sts remain. BO.

BACK LEGS (make 2)

Using US 5 (3.75mm) DPNs and **A**, CO 4 sts, PM, join to knit in the round.

Round 1: [Kfb] 4 times. (8 sts)

Round 2: [Kfb] 8 times. (16 sts)

Round 3: [K2, m1, k2] 4 times. (20 sts)

Round 4: [K1, m1, k3, m1, k6] twice. (24 sts)

Rounds 5 to 8: Knit.

Round 9: K5, k2tog, k5, k2tog, knit to end. (22 sts)

Round 10: K4, k2tog, k5, k2tog, knit to end. (20 sts)

Round 11: Knit.

Round 12: K1, m1, k1, k2tog, k7, k2tog, k1, m1, knit to end.

Rounds 13–17: Knit.

Round 18: K1, k2tog, k1, m1, k7, m1, k1, k2tog, knit to end.

Round 19: Knit.

Round 20: K4, m1, k7, m1, knit to end. (22 sts)

Round 21: Knit.

Round 22: K5, m1, k7, m1, knit to end. (24 sts)

Begin upper portion of leg.

Right leg

Round 23: BO7, knit to last 2 sts, k2tog, turn. Continue knitting in rows. (16 sts)

Row 24: P5, p2tog, p3, m1, p3, p2tog, p1. (15 sts)

Row 25: Knit to last 2 sts, k2tog. (14 sts)

Row 26: P9, m1, p3, p2tog.

Row 27: Knit to last 2 sts, k2tog. (13 sts)

Row 28: P3, p2tog, p4, m1, p2, p2tog. (12 sts)

Row 29: Knit to last 2 sts, k2tog. (11 sts)

Row 30: P8, m1, p1, p2tog.

Row 31: K1, k2tog, k5, k2tog, k1. (9 sts)

Row 32: Purl.

Row 33: K1, k2tog, k3, k2tog, k1. (7 sts)

Row 34: P1, p2tog, p1, p2tog, p1. (5 sts) BO.

Left leg

Round 23: K12, BO7, slip last st on right needle back to left needle, k2tog, k3. Remove marker. (16 sts)

Continue knitting in rows, working in the same direction as round 23 for the first row.

Row 24: K2tog, k4, m1, k4, k2tog. (15 sts)

Row 25: Purl to last 2 sts, p2tog. (14 sts)

Row 26: K9, m1, k3, k2tog.

Row 27: Purl to last 2 sts, p2tog. (13 sts)

Row 28: K3, k2tog, k4, m1, k2, k2tog. (12 sts)

Row 29: Purl to last 2 sts, p2tog. (11 sts)

Row 30: K8, m1, k1, k2tog.

Row 31: P1, p2tog, purl to last 3 sts, p2tog, p1. (9 sts)

Row 32: Knit.

Row 33: P1, p2tog, p3, p2tog, p1. (7 sts)

Row 34: K1, k2tog, k1, k2tog, k1. (5 sts) BO.

Stuff all 4 legs.

FRONT LEGS

BACK LEGS

EARS

EARS (make 2)

Using US 5 (3.75mm) DPNs and **A**, CO 10 sts, PM, join to knit in the round.

Rounds 1–3: Knit.

Round 4: [K2, m1, k3] twice. (12 sts)

Rounds 5–7: Knit.

Round 8: [K3, m1, k3] twice. (14 sts)

Rounds 9–10: Knit.

Round 11: [K3, m1, k4] twice. (16 sts)

Rounds 12–13: Knit.

Round 14: [K1, m1, k6, m1, k1] twice. (20 sts)

Rounds 15–16: Knit.

Round 17: K1, k2tog, k14, k2tog, k1. (18 sts)

Round 18: Knit.

Round 19: K7, place next 4 sts on scrap yarn, k7. (14 sts)

Rounds 20–22: Knit.

Round 23: [K2, k2tog, k3] twice. (12 sts)

Rounds 24 to 26: Knit.

Round 27: [K2, k2tog, k2] twice. (10 sts)

Round 28: Knit.

Round 29: [K1, k2tog, k2] twice. (8 sts)

Round 30: Knit.

Round 31: [K2tog] 4 times. (4 sts)

Round 32: [K2tog] twice. (2 sts)

Break yarn, pull tail through remaining sts, and pull loose end into inside of fabric.

Place sts from scrap yarn on US 5 (3.75mm) DPNs, join to knit in the round.

Using **A**, knit one round.

Next round: [K2tog] twice. (2 sts)

Break yarn, pull tail through remaining sts, and pull loose end into inside of fabric. Stuff ears lightly.

TAIL

Using US 5 (3.75mm) DPNs and **B**, CO 24 sts, PM, join to knit in the round.

Rounds 1–14: Knit.

Round 15: [K2tog, k4] 4 times. (20 sts)

Rounds 16–29: Knit.

Round 30: [K2tog, k3] 4 times. (16 sts)

Row 31: K11, wrap and turn.

Row 32: P10, wrap and turn.

Rounds 33–44: Knit.

Round 45: [K2tog, k2] 4 times. (12 sts)

Row 46: K8, wrap and turn.

Row 47: P7, wrap and turn.

Rounds 48–52: Knit.

Row 53: K8, wrap and turn.

Row 54: P7, wrap and turn.

Rounds 55–58: Knit.

Round 59: [K2tog, k1] 4 times. (8 sts)

Row 60: K5, wrap and turn.

Row 61: P4, wrap and turn.

Rounds 62–64: Knit.

Round 65: [K2tog] 4 times. (4 sts)

Round 66: Knit.

Round 67: [K2tog] twice. (2 sts)·

Break yarn, pull tail through remaining sts, and pull loose end into inside of fabric.

ASSEMBLY

Cut out all felt pieces using templates.

Use images as guides for positioning.

Glue inner ears to ears.

Glue paw pads to feet.

Embroider mouth and nose using **C**.

Sew ears to head.

Sew legs to body.

Sew tail base to body.

Tail: Using short strands of **B**, use a crochet hook to attach to tail, working from the top down. Use a felt brush or toothbrush to separate and brush out the strands as you go.

Collar: Starting just behind the neck, repeat same procedure as for tail, attaching strands of yarn in a 1in wide band, brushing into a clockwise swoop as you go.

Hair tuft: Using strands of **B**, attach to top of head in a small diamond shaped pattern. Repeat brushing technique as for tail and collar.

Be sure to weave in all ends to ensure a smooth finish.

TAIL

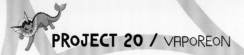

VAPOREON

OFFICIAL COLORS

NATIONAL POKÉDEX NO.	TYPE	WEIGHT	HEIGHT
0134	Water	63.9 lbs/ 29.0 kg	3 ft 3 in/ 1.0 m

Its cell composition is similar to water molecules. As a result, it can't be seen when it melts away into water.

MATERIALS

- Cascade 220 (100% wool), 10-ply/ aran, 100g (220yd/200m), in the following shades:
- Pacific (2433); 2 balls (**A**)
- Azure (8892); 110yd/100m (**B**)
- White (8505); 110yd/100m (**C**)
- Lemon Yellow (4147); 110yd/100m (**D**)
- Black (8555); Oddments (**E**)
- Blue embroidery floss
- Set of five size US 5 (3.75mm) DPNs
- Felt pieces in black, gray, and white
- Fabric glue
- Polyester filling

GAUGE

22 sts and 26 rows measure 4 x 4in (10 x 10cm) over stockinette stitch (stocking stitch) using US 5 (3.75mm) needles.

FINISHED SIZE

24in (61cm) long

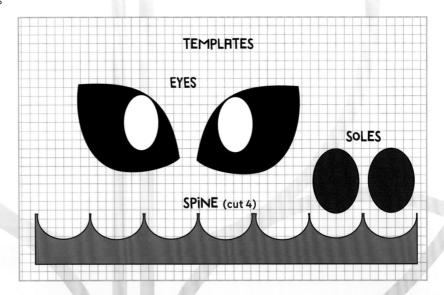

TEMPLATES

EYES

SOLES

SPINE (cut 4)

COLLAR (make 1 in A and 1 in C)

Using US 5 (3.75mm) DPNs, CO 42 sts, PM, join to knit in the round.

Rounds 1–2: Knit.

Round 3: [Kfb, k5] 7 times. (49 sts)

Rounds 4–5: Knit.

Round 6: [Kfb, k6] 7 times. (56 sts)

Rounds 7–8: Knit.

Round 9: (Kfb, k7) 7 times. (63 sts)

Rounds 10–11: Knit.

Round 12: [Kfb, k8] 7 times. (70 sts)

Rounds 13–14: Knit.

Round 15: [Kfb, k9] 7 times. (77 sts)

Rounds 16–17: Knit.

Round 18: [Kfb, k10] 7 times. (84 sts)

Rounds 19–20: Knit.

Create collar trim points:

Row 21: K2, k2tog, k2, turn.

Row 22: P2tog, p1, p2tog, turn.

Row 23: Sl1, k2tog, psso. Break yarn, pull tail through remaining st. Weave in loose ends.

Reattach working yarn to next st and repeat rounds 21–23 thirteen more times. Press collars lightly. Placing purl sides of fabric together, seam top and bottom edges. The white side should be the inside the flare. Press again once fully seamed. Set aside.

BODY (worked from the rear forward)

Using US 5 (3.75mm) DPNs and **A**, CO 4 sts, PM, join to knit in the round.

Round 1: [Kfb] 4 times. (8 sts)

Round 2: [Kfb] 8 times. (16 sts)

Round 3: Knit.

Round 4: [K1, m1, k2, m1, k1] 4 times. (24 sts)

Round 5: Knit.

Round 6: [K2, m1, k2, m1, k2] 4 times. (32 sts)

Round 7: Knit

Round 8: [K3, m1, k2, m1, k3] 4 times. (40 sts)

Round 9: Knit.

Round 10: [K3, m1, k4, m1, k3] 4 times. (48 sts)

Rounds 11–43: Knit.

Begin turn for chest:

Row 44: K35, wrap and turn.

Row 45: P34, wrap and turn.

Row 46: K33, wrap and turn.

Row 47: P32, wrap and turn.

Row 48: K31, wrap and turn.

Row 49: P30, wrap and turn.

Row 50: K29, wrap and turn.

Row 51: P28, wrap and turn.

Row 52: K27, wrap and turn.

Row 53: P26, wrap and turn.

Row 54: K25, wrap and turn.

Row 55: P24, wrap and turn.

Row 56: K23, wrap and turn.

Row 57: P22, wrap and turn.

Row 58: K21, wrap and turn.

Row 59: P20, wrap and turn.

Row 60: K19, wrap and turn.

Row 61: P18, wrap and turn.

Row 62: K17, wrap and turn.

Row 63: P16, wrap and turn.

Row 64: K15, wrap and turn.

Row 65: P14, wrap and turn, knit to end.

Rounds 66–67: Knit.

Round 68: K1, k2tog, k30, k2tog, knit to end. (46 sts)

Round 69: Knit.

Round 70: K1, k2tog, k28, k2tog, knit to end. (44 sts)

Rounds 71–72: Knit.

Round 73: [K12, k2tog, k4, k2tog, k2] twice. (40 sts)

Rounds 74–75: Knit.

Round 76: [K3, m1, k4, m1, k3] 4 times. (48 sts)

Round 77: Knit.

Round 78: [K3, m1, k6, m1, k3] 4 times. (56 sts)

Round 79: Knit.

COLLAR

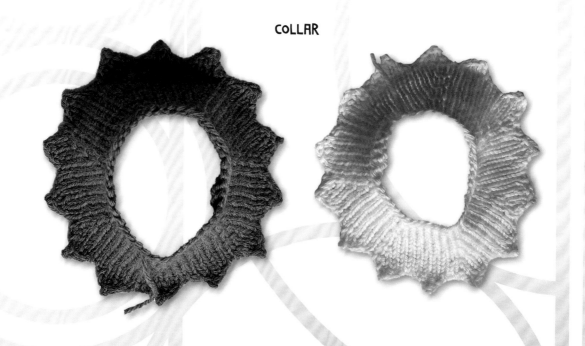

Stuff body.

Begin turn for head. Slip marker as you pass it.

Round 80: K13, wrap and turn.

Round 81: P40, wrap and turn.

Round 82: K38, wrap and turn.

Round 83: P36, wrap and turn.

Round 84: K34, wrap and turn.

Round 85: P32, wrap and turn.

Round 86: K30, wrap and turn.

Round 87: P28, wrap and turn.

Round 88: K26, wrap and turn.

Round 89: P24, wrap and turn.

Round 90: K22, wrap and turn.

Round 91: P20, wrap and turn.

Round 92: K18, wrap and turn.

Round 93: P16, wrap and turn.

Round 94: K14, wrap and turn.

Round 95: P12, wrap and turn.

Begin second turn, pick up and knit wraps as you go.

Round 96: K13, wrap and turn.

Round 97: P14, wrap and turn.

Round 98: K16, wrap and turn.

Round 99: P18, wrap and turn.

Round 100: K20, wrap and turn.

Round 101: P22, wrap and turn.

Round 102: K24, wrap and turn.

Round 103: P26, wrap and turn.

Round 104: K28, wrap and turn.

Round 105: P30, wrap and turn.

Round 106: K32, wrap and turn.

Round 107: P34, wrap and turn.

Round 108: K36, wrap and turn.

Round 109: P38, wrap and turn, knit to end.

Round 110: Knit.

Round 111: K3, k2tog, k12, k2tog, k4, k2tog, k12, k2tog, k6, k2tog, k4, k2tog, k3. (50 sts)

Round 112: Knit.

Round 113: K3, k2tog, k28, k2tog, knit to end. (48 sts)

Round 114: Knit.

Round 115: K3, k2tog, k10, k2tog, k2, k2tog, k10, k2tog, k6, k2tog, k2, k2tog, k3. (42 sts)

Round 116: Knit.

Round 117: K3, k2tog, k22, k2tog, knit to end. (40 sts)

Round 118: Knit.

Round 119: K3, k2tog, k7, k2tog, k2, k2tog, k7, k2tog, k5, k2tog, k2, k2tog, k2. (34 sts)

Round 120: Knit.

Round 121: K3, k2tog, k16, k2tog, knit to end. (32 sts)

Round 122: [K1, k2tog, k2, k2tog, k1] 4 times. (24 sts)

Slip collar over head and center on neck. You will stitch into place later. Stuff head.

Round 123: [K1, k2tog, k2tog, k1] 4 times. (16 sts)

Round 124: [K2tog] 8 times. (8 sts)

Round 125: [K2tog] 4 times. (4 sts)

Break yarn, pull tail through remaining sts, and pull loose end into inside of fabric.

FRONT LEGS (make 2)

Using US 5 (3.75mm) DPNs and **A**, CO 4 sts, PM, join to knit in the round.

Round 1: [Kfb] 4 times. (8 sts)

Round 2: [Kfb] 8 times. (16 sts)

Round 3: [Kfb, k1] 8 times. (24 sts)

Rounds 4–7: Knit.

Round 8: K5, k2tog, k5, k2tog, knit to end. (22 sts)

Round 9: K4, k2tog, k5, k2tog, knit to end. (20 sts)

Round 10: K3, k2tog, k5, k2tog, knit to end. (18 sts)

Round 11: Knit.

Round 12: K1, m1, k1, k2tog, k5, k2tog, k1, m1, knit to end.

Rounds 13–14: Knit.

Round 15: K1, m1, k1, k2tog, k5, k2tog, k1, m1, knit to end.

Rounds 16–17: Knit.

Round 18: K1, m1, k1, k2tog, k5, k2tog, k1, m1, knit to end.

Round 19: Knit.

Round 20: K1, k2tog, k1, m1, k7, m1, k1, k2tog, knit to end.

Rounds 21–22: Knit.

Round 23: K1, k2tog, k1, m1, k7, m1, k1, k2tog, knit to end.

Repeat rounds 21–23.

Round 27: Knit.

Begin upper portion of leg.

FRONT LEGS

BODY

Right leg

Round 28: BO4, knit to last 2 sts, k2tog, remove marker, knit to end. (13 sts)

Continue knitting in rows.

Row 29: P2tog, purl to end. (12 sts)

Row 30: K2tog, knit to end. (11 sts)

Repeat rows 29–30 until 5 sts remain. BO.

Left leg

Round 28: K9, BO 4 sts, slip last st on right needle back to left needle, k2tog, k3, remove marker. (13 sts)

Continue knitting in rows.

Row 29: Knit to last 2 sts, k2tog. (12 sts)

Row 30: Purl to last 2 sts, p2tog. (11 sts)

Repeat rows 29–30 until 5 sts remain. BO.

BACK LEGS (make 2)

Using US 5 (3.75mm) DPNs and **A**, CO 4 sts, PM, join to knit in the round.

Round 1: [Kfb] 4 times. (8 sts)

Round 2: [Kfb] 8 times. (16 sts)

Round 3: [Kfb, k1] 8 times. (24 sts)

Rounds 4–7: Knit.

Round 8: K5, k2tog, k5, k2tog, knit to end. (22 sts)

Round 9: K4, k2tog, k5, k2tog, knit to end. (20 sts)

Round 10: K3, k2tog, k5, k2tog, knit to end. (18 sts)

Round 11: Knit.

Round 12: K1, m1, k1, k2tog, k5, k2tog, k1, m1, knit to end.

Rounds 13–14: Knit.

Round 15: K1, m1, k1, k2tog, k5, k2tog, k1, m1, knit to end.

Rounds 16–17: Knit.

Round 18: K1, m1, k1, k2tog, k5, k2tog, k1, m1, knit to end.

Round 19: Knit.

Round 20: K3, m1, k7, m1, knit to end. (20 sts)

Round 21: Knit.

Round 22: K2tog, k2, m1, k7, m1, k2, k2tog, knit to end.

Round 23: Knit.

Round 24: K4, m1, k7, m1, knit to end. (22 sts)

Round 25: Knit.

Round 26: K2tog, k3, m1, k7, m1, k3, k2tog, knit to end.

Round 27: Knit.

Round 28: K5, m1, k7, m1, knit to end. (24 sts)

Round 29: Knit.

Round 30: K2tog, k4, m1, k7, m1, k4, k2tog, knit to end.

Round 31: Knit.

Round 32: K6, m1, k7, m1, knit to end. (26 sts_

Round 33: Knit.

Begin upper portion of leg.

Right leg

Round 34: BO 8 sts, knit to last 2 sts, k2tog. (17 sts)

Remove marker, continue knitting in rows.

Row 35: Purl to last 2 sts, p2tog. (16 sts)

Row 36: Knit to last 2 sts, k2tog. (15 sts)

Repeat rows 35–36 until you have 11 sts

Row 41: Purl to last 2 sts, p2tog. (10 sts)

Row 42: K2tog, k6, k2tog. (8 sts)

Row 43: Purl.

Row 44: K2tog, k4, k2tog. (6 sts)

BO.

Left leg

Round 34: K13, BO 8 sts, slip last st from right needle to left needle, k2tog, knit to end. (17 sts)

Remove marker, continue knitting in rows.

Row 35: Knit to last 2 sts, k2tog. (16 sts)

Row 36: Purl to last 2 sts, p2tog. (15 sts)

Repeat rows 35–36 until you have 11 sts

Row 41: Knit to last 2 sts, k2tog. (10 sts)

Row 42: P2tog, p6, p2tog. (8 sts)

Row 43: Knit.

Row 44: P2tog, p4, p2tog. (6 sts)

BO. Stuff all 4 legs.

BACK LEGS

PROJECT 20 / VAPOREON

HEAD TRIM

US 5 (3.75mm) DPNs and **B**, CO 8 sts.

Row 1 (RS): Knit.

Row 2: Purl.

Row 3: K2, m1, knit to last 2 sts, m1, k2. (10 sts)

Row 4: Purl.

Repeat rows 3–4 until you have 24 sts

Row 19: K2, k2tog, knit to last 4 sts, k2tog, k2. (22 sts)

Row 20: Purl.

Repeat rows 19–20 until you have 8 sts.

Row 35: K3, k2tog, k3. (7 sts)

Row 36: Purl.

Row 37: K3, k2tog, k2. (6 sts)

Row 38: Purl.

Row 39: K2, k2tog, k2. (5 sts)

Row 40: Purl.

Row 41: K2, k2tog, k1. (4 st)s

Row 42: Purl.

Row 43: K1, k2tog, k1. (3 sts)

Row 44: Sl, p2tog, psso. (1 st)

Break yarn, pull tail through remaining st,

TOP FIN

Using US 5 (3.75mm) DPNs and **D**, CO 28 sts, PM, join to knit in the round.

Round 1: K1, k2tog, knit to last 3 sts, k2tog, k1. (26 sts)

Round 2: K1, k2tog, knit to last 3 sts, k2tog, k1. (24 sts)

Round 3: Knit.

Round 4: [K1, k2tog, k6, k2tog, k1] twice. (20 sts)

Round 5: Knit.

Round 6: K1, k2tog, knit to last 3 sts, k2tog, k1. (18 sts)

Round 7: Knit.

Round 8: [K1, k2tog, k3, k2tog, k1] twice. (14 sts)

Round 9: K1, m1, k12, m1, k1. (16 sts)

Round 10: K1, m1, k14, m1, k1. (18 sts)

Round 11: Knit.

Round 12: K1, k2tog, knit to last 3 sts, k2tog, k1. (16 sts)

Round 13: Knit.

Round 14: K1, k2tog, k10, k2tog, k1. (14 sts)

Round 15: Knit.

Round 16: [K1, k2tog, k1, k2tog, k1] twice. (10 sts)

Round 17: Knit.

Round 18: [K2, k2tog] twice, k2. (8 sts0

Round 19: Knit.

Round 20: K2, k2tog twice, k2. (6 sts)

Round 21: Knit.

Round 22: [K2tog] 3 times. (3 sts)

Break yarn, pull tail through remaining sts. Weave in loose ends. Press flat. Do not stuff.

TOP FIN SPIKE

Using US 5 (3.75mm) DPNs and **A**, CO 7 sts.

Row 1 (RS): Knit.

Row 2: Purl.

Row 3: Knit.

Row 4: Purl.

Row 5: K3, k2tog, k2. (6 sts)

Row 6: Purl.

Row 7: Knit.

Row 8: Purl.

Row 9: Knit.

Row 10: Purl.

Row 11: K2, k2tog, k2. (5 sts)

Row 12: Purl.

Row 13: Knit.

Row 14: Purl.

Row 15: Knit.

Row 16: Purl.

Row 17: K1, k2tog, k2. (4 sts)

Row 18: Purl.

Row 19: Knit.

Row 20: Purl.

Row 21: Knit.

Row 22: Purl.

Row 23: K1, k2tog, k1. (3 sts)

Row 24: Purl.

Row 25: Knit.

Row 26: Purl.

Row 27: Sl, k2tog, psso. (1 st)

Break yarn, pull tail through remaining st.

Press lightly.

HEAD TRIM

TOP FIN

EARS (make 2)

Using US 5 (3.75mm) DPNs and **A**, CO 10 sts, PM, join to knit in the round.

Row 1 (RS): Knit.

Row 2: Purl.

Row 3: Knit.

Row 4: Purl.

Row 5: K4, k2tog, k4. (9 sts)

Row 6: Purl.

Row 7: Knit.

Row 8: Purl.

Row 9: K4, k2tog, k3. (8 sts)

Row 10: Purl.

Row 11: Knit.

Row 12: Purl.

Row 13: K3, k2tog, k3. (7 sts)

Row 14: Purl.

Row 15: Knit.

Row 16: Purl.

Row 17: K3, k2tog, k2. (6 sts)

Row 18: Purl.

Row 19: Knit.

Row 20: Purl.

Row 21: Knit.

Row 22: Purl.

Row 23: K2, k2tog, k2. (5 sts)

Row 24: Purl.

Row 25: Knit.

Row 26: Purl.

Row 27: Knit.

Row 29: Purl.

Row 30: K2, k2tog, k1. (4 sts)

Row 31: Purl.

Row 32: Knit.

Row 33: Purl.

Row 34: [K2tog] twice. (2 sts)

Break yarn, pull tail through remaining sts. Press lightly.

EAR FINS (make 2)

Using US 5 (3.75mm) DPNs and **D**, CO 10 sts, PM, join to knit in the round.

Rounds 1–2: Knit.

Round 3: [K1, m1, k3, m1, k1] twice. (14 sts)

Rounds 4–6: Knit.

Round 7: [K1, m1, k5, m1, k1] twice. (18 sts)

Rounds 8–10: Knit.

Round 11: [K1, m1, k7, m1, k1] twice. (22 sts)

Rounds 12–14: Knit.

Round 15: [K1, m1, k9, m1, k1] twice. (26 sts)

Rounds 16: Knit.

Round 17: K22, BO 4 sts. (22 sts)

Round 18: BO 4 sts (1 st left on right needle from BO), k17. (18 sts)

Round 19: K2tog, k6, m1, k2, m1, k6, k2tog.

Round 20: K16, BO2. (16 sts)

Round 21: BO 2 sts (1 st left on right needle from BO), k13. (14 sts)

Round 22: K2tog, k10, k2tog. (12 sts)

Round 23: K5, m1, k2, m1, k5. (14 sts)

Round 24: Knit.

Round 25: K12, BO 2 sts. (12 sts)

Round 26: BO 2 sts (1 st left on right needle from BO), k9. (10 sts)

Round 27: K2tog, k2, m1, k2, m1, k2, k2tog.

Round 28: Knit.

Round 29: K2tog, k6, k2tog. (8 sts)

Round 30: Knit.

Round 31: K2tog, k4, k2tog. (6 sts)

Round 32: [K2tog] 3 times. (3 sts_

Break yarn, pull tail through remaining sts. Weave in loose end. Close holes from bound off sts. Press lightly. Do not stuff.

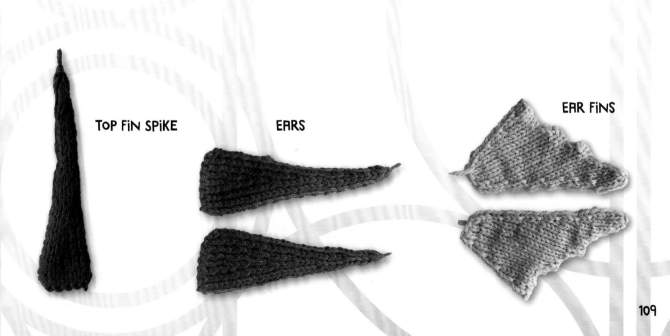

TOP FIN SPIKE · EARS · EAR FINS

TAIL

Using US 5 (3.75mm) DPNs and **A**, CO 40 sts, PM, join to knit in the round.

Rounds 1–14: Knit.

Round 15: [K2tog, k8] 4 times. (36 sts)

Rounds 16–29: Knit.

Round 30: [K2tog, k7] 4 times. (32 sts)

Rounds 31–44: Knit.

Round 45: [K2tog, k6] 4 times. (28 sts)

Rounds 46–59: Knit.

Round 60: [K2tog, k5] 4 times. (24 sts)

Rounds 61–74: Knit.

Round 75: [K2tog, k4) 4 times. (20 sts)

Rounds 76–89: Knit.

Round 90: [K2tog, k3] 4 times. (16 sts)

Rounds 91–94: Knit.

Round 95: [K2tog, k2] 4 times. (12 sts)

Rounds 96–99: Knit.

Round 100: [K2tog, k1] 4 times. (8 sts)

Round 101: [K2tog] 4 times. (4 sts)

Break yarn, pull tail through remaining sts. Weave in loose end. Stuff tail.

TAIL FINS (make 2)

Using US 5 (3.75mm) DPNs and **A**, CO 6 sts, PM, join to knit in the round.

Round 1: [Kfb, kfb, k1] twice. (10 sts)

Round 2: Knit.

Round 3: [K1, m1, k3, m1, k1] twice. (14 sts)

Round 4: Knit.

Round 5: [K1, m1, k5, m1, k1] twice. (18 sts)

Round 6: Knit.

Round 7: [K1, m1, k7, m1, k1] twice. (22 sts)

Round 8: Knit.

Round 9: [K1, m1, k9, m1, k1] twice. (26 sts)

Rounds 10–19: Knit.

Round 20: [K1, k2tog, k7, k2tog, k1] twice. (22 sts)

Round 21: Knit.

Round 22: [K1, k2tog, k5, k2tog, k1] twice. (18 sts)

Round 23: Knit.

Round 24: [K1, k2tog, k3, k2tog, k1] twice. (14 sts)

Round 25: Knit.

Round 26: [K1, k2tog, k1, k2tog, k1] twice. (10 sts)

Round 27: Knit.

Round 28: [K2tog, k1, k2tog] twice. (6 sts)

Round 29: [K2tog] 3 times. (3 sts)

Break yarn, pull tail through remaining sts. Weave in loose end. Do not stuff.

ASSEMBLY

Cut out all felt pieces using templates.

Use images as guides for positioning.

Glue felt pieces for eyes and soles of back feet.

Using yarn **E**, sew two ½in (1.5cm) lines on face in the shape of an upside **V**.

Use yarn **E** to embroider nose.

Use yarn **E** to sew lines on inside of collar.

Use yarn **D** to sew lines on ear fins, ¼in (0.75cm) apart.

Sew head trim to top of head.

Sew tail to body.

Sew tail fins to side of the tail tip.

Sew legs to bottom of body.

Sew ears to tops of ear fins.

Sew ears and fins to sides of head.

Sew top fin spike to front edge of top fin.

Sew top fin to top of head.

Sew head trim and neck collar into place.

Use matching embroidery floss to yarn **A**, sew sections of spine along back and tail.

Be sure to weave in all ends to ensure a smooth finish.

TAIL FINS

TAIL